Rude
Science

**Everything You've
Always Wanted to Know
About the Science No
One Ever Talks About**

Stefan Gates

Hardie Grant

QUADRILLE

To my fantastic Dad, Eric Gates.

For making me curious.

Contents

Chapter 01:
Hello

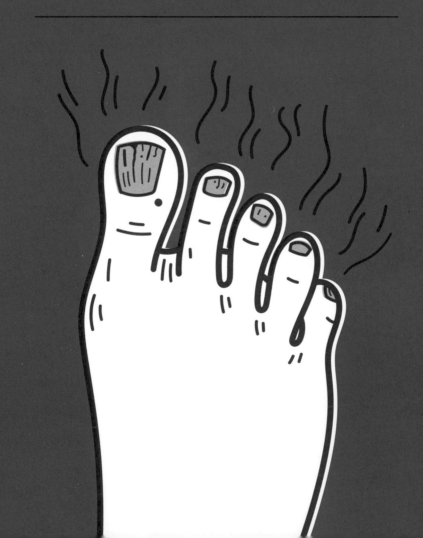

01.01
Hello, you
beautiful human

Welcome to the crispy, slimy, noisy, lumpy, smelly but absolutely vital science of you. We're taught from a young age to be ashamed of our biology and its quirks, but shame is a weapon that society uses to keep us in our place, to limit our happiness and repress our ambition. It's time to rebel against insidious embarrassment and fall in love with our bodies. I love your zits, your body odour, your warts, pus, farts and toe cheese, the various slimes, gloops and mucus you ooze, and the scabs, dander and scrofulous offcuts that your body constantly sheds.

This book is a celebration of your imperfections, quirks, boils and wrinkles as well as the alien world of microbes and parasites that live alongside you. I'm sure that you have a gorgeous face, handsome fingers, on-point hair and flawless skin, but these surface features are merely gifted to you – briefly – by the fickle hands of fate, genes and fashion. They're distractions from what makes you interesting. It's the quirky bits, the bits that aren't perfect, the bits that poets don't write about, that make you the complex, unique, multi-dimensional, perfectly imperfect individual you are.

And after all, without farts, vomit, spots, pus and pee, you simply wouldn't be alive.

So, of course, the title of this book is a paradox. Humans (including me) find bodily functions cripplingly embarrassing because we've been told to, and yet saying that any of our biology is 'rude' is as ridiculous as saying 'physics is angry'. Biology doesn't have a moral compass or sense of propriety any more than my shed does, and it doesn't care whether you like it or not – it just is. I've titled this book *Rude Science* not because I want you to think any of it is rude, but the opposite: I want to start setting us free from our embarrassment so that we start seeing the beauty within.

It's tragic, yet very human, that we are mortified by biological facts we have no control over. But if we discussed them more openly, perhaps we might be more comfortable in our skin. We might realize that there's no such thing as a freak – just wonderful difference. I don't expect everyone to start discussing the Bristol Stool Chart over dinner immediately but perhaps this book will give a small nudge in the right direction. And if there's a chance of it helping us love ourselves – and each other – a little more, isn't it worth a try?

I haven't explored the extraordinary world of diseases in any great detail here because there are already many excellent books about them, and in any case, my main aim is to make us less embarrassed about the ordinary things our bodies do that most books *don't* explore. The pathologies I do delve into are predominantly the ones that the vast majority of people are likely to experience, such as acne, scabs, pus and verrucas. While usually small problems, they can feel big at the time because we've been taught that they aren't welcome in polite society. It's time to bring our rashes out into the open.

Despite the embarrassment and revulsion that we all – me included – feel about some of this stuff, **the truth is there's no such thing as 'rude science', just science we haven't made friends with yet.**

Medical Note

It ought to go without saying that nothing in this book should be considered medical advice, and that if you have any concerns about your health, you should consult a doctor, not a quirkologist.

1.02 The sweet, sweet numbers of you

Your body is a beautiful sack of 7,000,000,000,000,000, 000,000,000,000 atoms packed into 30 trillion cells that are meticulously assembled – and then relentlessly broken apart and reassembled – into the shape of you according to the plans of your unique genetic blueprint. We are all different, which means that each of us is the most special of the 100 billion (also most special) people who have lived and died in the last 50,000 years, and with whom you share 99.5% of your DNA.

Your body is a busy chemistry lab, frantically anabolizing (building) and catabolizing (dismantling) all manner of juices, gases, proteins, carbs, fats and cells day and night from the nutrients you eat and drink via a spectacularly complex sequence of trillions of biochemical chemical reactions. Any number of these might be happening at any one time. In fact, **you are replacing most of your various cells so often that your body is, on average, only 15 years old**. This vast factory of biochemical reactions taking place inside you is collectively known as metabolism, and it's all plotted and controlled by your DNA, which contains the code for building proteins that create biological structures or make enzymes.

That code creates you: a combination of 64% water, 16% protein, 15% fat, 4% minerals and 1% carbohydrates. Using these, together with nutrition from your food and drink, you build 1.5 litres (2.6 pints) of saliva, 535ml (almost 1 pint) of sweat, 1.2 litres (2.2 pints) of snot, 1.6 litres (2.8 points) of urine, 2.4 million red blood cells, 150g (5oz) of faeces, 2.5 litres (4.4 pints) gastric juice, 1ml (0.04fl oz) of tears, and you shed 1.4g (0.05oz) of dead skin cells every day.

You also take 11,000 breaths, blink 15,000 times and generate 1.5 litres (2.6 pints) of flatus, expelled in 10–15 farts. These are produced by 200g (7oz) of bacteria in your gut. You have 5 million hairs, although only 100,000–150,000 of these are on your head. They grow 0.4mm (0.02in) every day and are closely related to your nails, which grow 3.5mm (0.14in) a month on your fingers and 1.6mm (0.06in) a month on your toes.

And while we're kicking numbers around, let's not forget that you have 5.5 litres (10 pints) of blood sloshing around inside you, travelling down 100,000km (62,000 miles – yes, you read that correctly) of veins and capillaries. It's all pushed around by your heart, which pumps about 6,200 litres (11,000 pints) through your body every day via 100,000 heartbeats. And just for good numerical measure, if you laid all the DNA in your body end to end, it would stretch 16 billion km (10 billion miles).

There are 78 organs in the body, 206 bones in adults (but over 300 in babies), over 600 muscles, two hairless nipples and one vestigial tail. And how much are you worth? Well, I'd say you're priceless, but in 2013 the Royal Society of Chemistry worked out how much it would cost to build a human from scratch using the purest forms of all the constituent elements. It came out at a whopping £96,546.79 ($127,000) for materials alone.

Chapter 02:
Juices, Gloops
& Crispy Bits

2.01 You are juicy

Your body uses about 2.5 litres (4.5 pints) of water a day but only two-thirds of that comes from the liquid you drink. A surprising 22% comes from the food you eat, and an even more surprising 12% is metabolic water produced as a by-product of burning fuel in your cells* (in the same way that a car produces mainly carbon dioxide and water – alongside a few unpleasant pollutants – when it burns petrol).

In total you're about 60% water but women are significantly drier than men, with a total body water proportion of 52–55% compared with men's 60–67%. Within the sexes, water proportion also differs on an individual basis, mainly as a result of your percentage of body fat (the more fat you carry, the lower proportion of water you have). Your brain is very wet indeed at 75–80% water plus a scattering of fat and protein. Either way, you are made of more water than any other substance**.

Too much water can kill you, though, proving that the famous Swiss physician Paracelsus (known as the father of toxicology) was correct when he said: 'all things are poisons, and the degree of toxicity is only caused by the dose'. Many people believe you need to

*Similarly, camels don't store water in their humps, but even so, they are a source of hydration. The hump is a soft, Spam-like fatty tissue that's metabolized in order to create water.

**If you're interested in the detail – and I'm delighted if you are – body fluid can be broken down into two types. Two-thirds is intracellular fluid held in your cells, and one-third is extracellular fluid, which sloshes around outside your cells in several ways: as interstitial fluid in the lymphatic system and in the spaces between cells (between cell membranes and skin, for instance), as blood plasma and as cerebrospinal fluid.

drink 2 litres (3.5 pints) of water every day, but this is not something most nutritionists advise – they just say 'keep well-hydrated'. In fact you should be careful not to drink too much water too quickly because it can cause water intoxication. This is when the water you drink dilutes the electrolytes in your body too fast for it to rebalance them. People have died from water intoxication, including a young Californian woman who drank 6 litres (10.6 pints) of water in three hours while taking part in a water-drinking contest run by a radio station. In 1995 an 18-year-old British schoolgirl died after taking an ecstasy tablet. Her death, however, was caused by her drinking 7 litres (12.3 pints) of water in less than 90 minutes.

2.02 Snot & bogies

You produce (and swallow*) nasal mucus, or snot, throughout the day, making 1–1.5 litres (1.8–2.6 pints) of the stuff every 24 hours. Snot is a clever, sticky gel made in the nasal cavity, mouth and throat, and its main job is to catch foreign particles, such as dust, bacteria and viruses, as they swirl around your airways. **You breathe in around 8,500 litres (15,000 pints) of air every day** and that air is packed with tiny particulates and microbes that could damage your delicate lungs, so snot provides a hugely important line of defence. After oozing out, this sticky concoction slithers along to your pharynx using a fascinating transport system called mucociliary clearance, after which you either swallow and destroy it in the tough, acidic gastric juices in your stomach or (more rarely) cough or sneeze it up.

Snot is 95% water, but its jelly-like consistency derives from the 2–3% of large glycoprotein mucin molecules secreted by mucous glands and cells. These extraordinary mucins are made up of very large molecules, and the strands, threads and sheets they form bind water together in a gloopy, viscous, cross-linked semi-solid gel**. The rest of the snot is made up of small amounts of proteoglycans, lipids, proteins and DNA.

Mucociliary clearance ranks alongside peristalsis and cycling as one of my favourite transport methods. After mopping up the muck

*Incidentally, you swallow about 2,000 times a day – about once every 30 seconds.

**Gels are fascinating – they are substances that are mostly liquid but behave like solids because of a cross-linked network. Interestingly, the word 'gel' was coined in the 19th century as a shortening of the word 'gelatine' by the Scottish colloid chemist Thomas Graham.

you breathe in, the snot is slowly moved towards your pharynx by millions of microscopic, hair-like cilia that beat around 16 times every second and push it along at a rip-roaring speed of 6–20mm (0.2–0.8in) per minute.

For all the good snot does, it also causes problems by providing a safe, damp haven for some viruses that would swiftly die without it. **A Swiss study found that the flu virus can only survive on a banknote for a few hours – unless it's joined by a microdot of snot, in which case it can last for two and a half weeks**.

So when does snot become a bogey? Well, as every school kid knows, bogies are harder, drier and eminently more flickable than snot. The mucous near the opening of your nose is liable to dry out as a result of greater evaporation there than in the rest of the respiratory tract. This can make it too thick for mucociliary clearance to work, so it becomes a thick clump of desiccated gel (preferably crispy on the outside, soft on the inside, IMHO). At this point a clean exploratory finger may need to be deployed. Research carried out in

---

Snotology

Why are bogies green? Well, snot is normally a relatively thin and clear gel, but illness can make it thicker and turn it yellow or green as a result of an antibacterial enzyme called myeloperoxidase that's secreted by your white blood cells to tackle infection.

Wisconsin indicated that around 91% of people pick their nose (or at least, only 91% admitted to it) and one person in the study spent 1–2 hours per day at it. Another study in Bangalore found that **most adolescents admitted to picking their nose four times a day and that 20% of them thought they had a 'serious nose-picking problem'. Twelve per cent said they picked their nose simply because they enjoyed it**.

Which brings us to the question you've all been desperate to ask: is rhinotillexic mucophagy okay? In other words, is it safe to pick, then eat your bogies? Well, in 2004 Austrian lung specialist Professor Friedrich Bischinger said that eating your bogies was good for the immune system (after all, you'd probably have swallowed them anyway by mucociliary clearance). There's no research to back this up but as long as your finger is clean, there shouldn't be too much of a problem. Do be careful not to hurt your nose with over-enthusiastic bogey-mining, though.

2.03 Phlegm

Phlegm is a wonderful word, both on paper and in the mouth, but in the lungs it's a gloopy gel similar to snot. Both are mucuses oozed from your mucous membranes but whereas snot lines the nose, throat and mouth, phlegm is produced in the lungs, mostly when you're ill. When we do that 'harruaargh', cough-like noise to clear our lungs of muck, the jellified gloop that pops up is phlegm, and once it's mixed with saliva in the mouth, it's known as sputum.

Phlegmology

Just as snot moves down your throat via mucociliary clearance, phlegm makes its way up your throat using the 'ciliary escalator', the wave-like movement of tiny cilia hairs lining the throat and lungs, and can also be helped on its way by coughing (see p58). The mucus stimulates nerve receptors in the lungs and throat, making us cough, and forcing the phlegm out along with a blast of air. Once the flob of phlegm (along with whatever muck it's carrying) arrives in the larynx, it's out of the sensitive airways and can be directed either into the mouth for spitting into a tissue (known as 'expectorating' if you're posh) or, far more likely, swallowed into the stomach, where your acidic gastric juices break it down and destroy any dangerous substances.

Healthy people only produce a tiny amount of phlegm: just 15–50ml (0.5–1.8fl oz) every day. But when you're ill the phlegm factory kicks in. How much your mucous membranes ramp up production depends on your illness, but **if you're unfortunate enough to get bronchorrhoea, you can produce up to 2 litres (3.5 pints) of phlegm a day. That's a lot of gloop**.

Phlegm is produced as a defence mechanism to trap and remove dangerous substances from our lungs, and the base ingredients are similar to those of snot: water, gelling agents, proteins and salts, along with antibodies and enzymes. The colour can be anything from green to red, yellow, brown or even black, depending on the extra toppings thrown in by whatever has triggered the phlegm in the first place: a cold, bronchitis, flu, or from inhaling smoke or dust. You can learn a lot about the root problem by taking a close look: transparent phlegm usually indicates a virus but white or yellow phlegm can mean it's mixed with pus, hinting at a bacterial infection. Green suggests a specific bacterial infection, red indicates bleeding, and black hints that you've inhaled particles such as coal dust. And although it's a defence mechanism, phlegm can cause a lot of problems to people who have respiratory issues, making breathing difficult.

2.04 Earwax

Earwax is another of those bodily gloops that thoroughly disgusts us, despite being vital to our health. Formally known as cerumen, it's a slightly bitter-tasting (well, mine is) mixture of keratin (60%) from old skin cells and hair held together by oils (12–20%) that include sticky sebum secreted by the sebaceous glands in our hair follicles, along with less sticky secretions from specialized ceruminous sweat glands found in our outer ear canal. It also has varying amounts of squalene, alcohols and cholesterol.

This waxy antibacterial mixture protects the ear canal in various ways: it waterproofs the ear's skin and keeps it lubricated and supple; it kills some bacteria and fungi; and it coats the guard hairs of the ear so that some unwelcome intruders such as dust and bacteria stick to these rather than entering the ear's delicate interior.

Interestingly, **there are two types of earwax, wet and dry, and the likelihood of you having one or the other is determined by your genes**. The more common wet type contains more oils and has a yellow-to-brown colour, and you're most likely to have it if you're African or European. You're more likely to have the grey and flaky dry type if you're Native American, East Asian or South-East Asian. Research has also shown that wet-waxers tend to produce underarm body odour, but dry-waxers much less so.

Whilst we all love hoiking a fingerful of earwax out with a clean finger, you shouldn't because the ears have a fascinating natural conveyor-belt mechanism to clear themselves, known as epithelial migration. The cells of the tympanic membrane (the barrier that seals and protects the middle ear) grow outwards at around the same pace as your fingernails do, making it more likely that debris ends up out rather than in, a process that is helped by your natural jaw movements.

But as we all know, our ears sometimes need a little help, and if this is the case, do NOT jam cotton buds down your lug holes or muck about with pointless (and dangerous) 'ear candling'. This practice of lighting a candle and putting the other end in your ear canal is highly likely to burn you or push earwax further down your ear and make the problem worse. Don't stick anything else in there either – my doctor once told me that **you shouldn't put anything smaller than your elbow in your ear, as it'll only do more harm than good**. Instead, trot along to your GP and ask them to take a look inside. If you really are suffering from cerumen impaction, they'll likely prescribe you a softener to lubricate the earwax and make it more mobile.

If you're lucky, your doctor will deem your blockage worthy of irrigating with warm water. I once had the pleasure of having an ear irrigated, and I would happily pay large sums of money to experience it again. My doctor used a little jet irrigation machine that pushed gentle pulses of pressurized water into my ear until the wax plug moved. And, oh my GOD! The feeling when the blockage finally shifted with a vast 'GLUG' was quite the knee-trembler.

2.05 Vomit

You produce 2–3 litres (3.5–5.3 pints) of gastric juice every day through various cells in the gastric glands lodged deep in your stomach lining. It's extremely acidic stuff with a pH of around 1–3 (somewhere between battery acid and vinegar), which is why you get a strong, lingering sour taste in your mouth when you call Huey down the great white telephone*. But as with so many human juices, it's a fascinating cocktail to explore, not least because you can cook food in it (see Vomology, opposite).

It also contains the intriguingly named 'intrinsic factor' (which we use to absorb vitamin B12), hormones including gastrin, the enzyme pepsinogen (which tastes nothing like Pepsi™, disappointingly), water and salts. All in all, it's a pretty caustic concoction to have sloshing around inside us, which is why we also secrete a sticky, alkaline mucus that lines the stomach to stop the acid burning holes in it. Of course, vomit is a combination of all these things, along with the partially mashed food and drink that we've guzzled, and these are collectively known as chyme** (pronounced 'kime').

*Puke

**It's unclear why we never say 'Oh God, I'm about to chyme', though there's an undeniable onomatopoeic heft to 'chunder', 'puke', 'vom', 'barf' and 'spew'.

***I did exactly this for a TV documentary in which we wanted to extract various E numbers from my body, including pure hydrochloric acid (E507).

<u>Vomology</u>

Gastric juice has many uses, but my favourite is that it effectively re-cooks your food. If you vomit up a cup of pure gastric juice*** (which is a bit tricky because an empty stomach only contains around 30ml (1fl oz) of the stuff – your gastric glands only really start producing it after food arrives), you will find that you can cook an egg in it. Crack the egg in and the white of it slowly turns opaque as the acid denatures its proteins in much the same way that the heat in a frying pan would. The Peruvian dish *ceviche* uses an identical cooking process involving lime juice: raw fish soaked in lime juice turns opaque as the proteins denature and surface bacteria are killed. Add milk to the gastric juice and you'll see that it curdles straight away. Don't you dare eat or drink any of this.

But gastric juice isn't just for fun – it also serves a vital function in killing many of the billions of microbes you've eaten alongside your food that can cause infections such as salmonella, cholera, dysentery and typhoid. It helps to kill the bacteria and fungal spores stuck in the 1–1.5 litres (1.8–2.6 pints) of snot you produce and swallow every day (see p13). It also helps to break down muscle fibres and connective tissue in meat and fish, helps pepsin enzymes to do their work, and helps you absorb calcium and iron.

2.06 Regurgitation

E*mesis* is the dramatic and noisy act of vomiting, rather than the slop of food and gastric juices that make up the stuff itself. Babies are particularly skilled at it – I have some excellent video footage of my super-cute four-week-old daughter Daisy sucking adorably on my nose before forcefully vomiting straight up it. This eruption of rancid slop from your stomach and duodenum (part of the small intestine that comes just after the stomach) is a useful 'better-out-than-in' reflex for getting rid of unwanted matter.

The mechanics of vomiting are fascinating. The triggers can be gastric problems (often the stomach responding after detecting contaminated food), bad smells and travel sickness. These can stimulate feelings of both nausea (a feeling of sickness) and anorexia (loss of appetite*). You then experience a complex set of motor responses that you have no control over: a sudden increase in production of particularly watery saliva in your mouth, sweating, dizziness, increased heart rate, pupil dilation and a narrowing of blood vessels in the skin (which is why sick people often look 'pale'). Your body is bracing itself for action.

Just before the vomit starts shooting upwards, you begin retching, which feels like very strong hiccups. Then **breathing becomes restricted as both your larynx and nasopharynx close to make sure that the anticipated acidic mixture doesn't enter your lungs (which would be extremely dangerous)**. Then the

*Strictly speaking, anorexia simply refers to loss of appetite, whereas the eating disorder is known as 'anorexia nervosa', but is often shortened to 'anorexia'.

stomach relaxes as the duodenum contracts, squirting any food that's started moving into the small intestine back into the stomach.

Next, the diaphragm and abdominal wall squeeze to build up pressure, the tap at the bottom of the stomach (the pyloric sphincter) closes, and finally the tap at the start of the stomach (the gastro-oesophageal sphincter) opens – and you're good to go! The pressure is released upwards, causing the stomach contents to shoot up the throat and out into (hopefully) a waiting bucket or toilet.

That's not quite the end of it. Your body may run the process again if it decides you need a really good clear-out. But as you relax the pressure is released and endorphins enter your bloodstream to make you feel better.

Being sick isn't the worst thing in the world but if you're already feeling ill, repeated regurgitation can be distressing and exhausting.

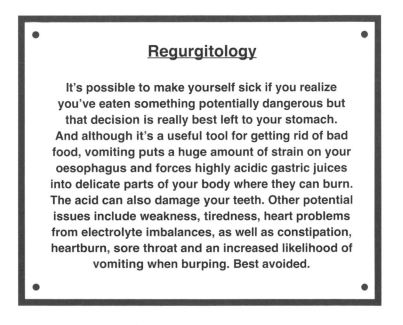

Regurgitology

It's possible to make yourself sick if you realize you've eaten something potentially dangerous but that decision is really best left to your stomach. And although it's a useful tool for getting rid of bad food, vomiting puts a huge amount of strain on your oesophagus and forces highly acidic gastric juices into delicate parts of your body where they can burn. The acid can also damage your teeth. Other potential issues include weakness, tiredness, heart problems from electrolyte imbalances, as well as constipation, heartburn, sore throat and an increased likelihood of vomiting when burping. Best avoided.

2.07 Pus

Yup, THIS is what you bought the book for. Whatever you think about bogies, wax and vom (which I hope you're beginning to fall in love with), pus inhabits an entirely different universe of revolting. So, brace your legs, people: we're going there.

Pus is a mesmerizing slop of dead white blood cells created during a battle between your body's defence system and pathogenic bacteria that are trying to infect you. Pathogenic means 'an organism that can cause disease' and bacteria are tiny living organisms, often made of just one biological cell. Not all bacteria are bad – in fact lots of them are essential, especially the 100 trillion that live in your gut and help you to digest food (see p123) – but the bad ones include those that cause cholera, anthrax, bubonic plague and salmonella. Cuts and grazes can be infected with lots of different types of bacteria but the most common are enterococci and staphylococci, which are found in nearly half of wound infections.

The story of pus follows a clear path: 1. Exposure. 2. Adhesion. 3. Invasion. 4. Colonization. 5. Toxicity. 6. Tissue damage and disease. First comes exposure. Bacteria (or fungi, parasites or prions) get into the body through an entry point – usually one of the heavily guarded human holes, such as the mouth, nose, bum, mucous membranes (eyes, penis or vagina – any part of your body that's kept moist by mucus) or a hole made by a cut in your skin. The vast majority of bacteria are killed, neutralized or simply removed as soon as they show up. But occasionally they arrive in high enough numbers, or are particularly dangerous. If the bacteria manage to adhere to and then invade cells, they can find a 'reservoir' where they

Pusology

When a collection of pus is under the skin and can't be seen, the gap it fills is called an abscess. When it is visible under the skin, it's called a pustule (zits, see p72, are pustules). The pus we mostly see after squeezing zits is yellowish but, depending on the type of bacteria your neutrophils were sent out to kill, it can also be green, brown or black. The green colour comes from either the vividly green myeloperoxidase enzyme the neutrophils use to kill the bacteria, or from a green pigment called pyocyanin that some bacteria produce to defend themselves from neutrophils. Green pus and most pus from anaerobic infections that don't involve oxygen are the types most likely to have a revolting smell.

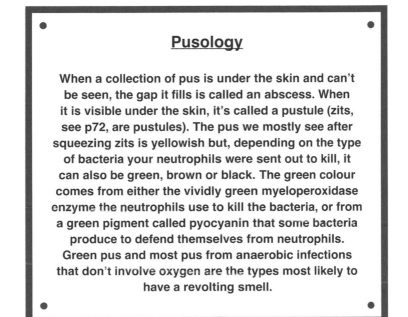

can live, grow and reproduce by feeding on our body's resources and colonization begins, which can lead to toxicity as the bacteria release toxins, followed by tissue damage and disease.

We haven't even got to the pus stage yet, but don't worry, it's on its way. As bacteria grow they can release toxins and destructive enzymes that cause damage. Special types of white cells called macrophages (or 'big-eaters': macro = big, phage = eater) constantly patrol your body looking for these bad bacteria, cancer cells and any other dangerous intruders, and when they stumble across them they engulf and eat them. Brutal stuff. These macrophages also release chemicals that attract other types of white blood cells within minutes, mostly ones called neutrophils, which are protein-rich and digest bacteria and fungi using enzymes*. Although this happens on a microscopic scale, you can feel and see this in your body as inflammation: a combination of swelling, redness, pain, heat and loss of function that's all part of the defensive process.

And here comes the pus. **The neutrophils tackle bad bacteria using a combination of three methods: they create a fibrous net to trap pathogens, they ooze a variety of antibacterial toxins and, most dramatically, they engulf bacteria and eat them**. Once the neutrophils' enzymes are all used up, they have completed the task they were designed for and die. In high enough concentrations this soup of exhausted dead neutrophils are a protein-rich gloop of dead cells we call pus.

*If you do a quick search, I can guarantee a happy afternoon watching extraordinary videos of neutrophils eating bacteria and fungi.

2.08 Spit

You ooze about 1.5 litres (2.6 pints) of spit every day from your salivary glands, creating about 40,000 litres of the stuff over a lifetime, although much of that is recycled. Salivary glands are found all over the mouth but are concentrated in three paired patches on either side. Weirdly, each pair produces different types of saliva. Behind the jaw but in front of the ears, the parotid glands produce 25% of your saliva, but it's a very watery, mucus-free version. Under the front of the tongue, the sublingual glands contribute a tiny 5% of total saliva, but it's a more viscous, rich and sticky variety. The submandibular glands under the back of the tongue make the vast majority (70%) of it, and their output consists of both types.

Saliva is 99% water*, helping to moisten and dilute food in your mouth. But it also contains small amounts of dissolved inorganic ions and organic components (mostly protein), as well as remarkably effective enzymes such as amylase and ptyalin, which start the chemical breakdown of food right there in your mouth.

As well as kick-starting the digestive process in your mouth, saliva helps to keep your teeth healthy and dissolves some substances in food to allow you to taste them. It contains bacteria-killing substances such as lysozyme and lactoferrin, and a fat-breaking enzyme called lipase. It also keeps the delicate surfaces of your pretty little mouth moist and supple and coats your teeth in a thin film of slimy mucins, which makes it easier to speak, chew and swallow.

*As all school kids know, the only way to win a spitting competition is to combine watery saliva together with a good doink of snot to give your flob a bit of body.

EXPERIMENT 1

SPITOLOGY

Here's a fascinating experiment you can use to demonstrate the power of amylase in your spit. Make up some Bird's Instant Custard (yes, it must be Bird's and yes, it must be instant) using boiling water, and let it cool for 30 minutes. Then take two identical glasses and put around 50ml (1.8fl oz) of cold custard in each. Spit about 10 good flobs of saliva into one of the glasses (ask a friend to contribute if you like) and stir it in. Add around 1 full teaspoon of water to the second glass (basically the same volume as you spat into the first glass), which is your control custard, and stir this in too. In the sink, prop a chopping board or plate up at a 45° angle and take both glasses of custard. Pour them both down the angled board and you should see that the custard with spit in it has become thin and runny whereas the custard with water is still thick and gloopy. This is because the amylase in your spit has broken apart the complex cornstarch molecules that kept the custard thick and gloopy. Probably best not to lick the bowl clean.

If that's too gross for you, suck on a piece of potato. If you do it for long enough, the enzymes in your spit slowly break the complex carbohydrates down into simpler sugars that you can taste on your tongue. Basically the potato begins to taste sweet.

2.09 Blood

The average human has 5.5 litres (9.7 pints) of blood sloshing around inside them – 70ml (2.5fl oz) or so for every kilogram (2.2lb) of body weight. Although blood is a complex mix of ingredients, you can break it down into two main parts: plasma fluid (55%), which is mostly water, and cells (45%) – mostly red blood cells, plus a much smaller proportion of white blood cells and platelets. Blood is moved around on a vast network of arteries, veins and capillaries that, if you laid them out end to end, would stretch 40,000–100,000km (25,000–62,000 miles). **Your heart beats just over once a second, which adds up to 100,000 heartbeats** pumping 6,200 litres (11,000 pints) of blood through your system every day.

Plasma – 55%

This is blood's liquid base, within which all the other ingredients are suspended. Think of it as the lorry that delivers the goods around the body. It's a light yellow colour and is 92% water, plus salts, nutrients from food (such as amino acids, glucose and fatty acids), carbon dioxide, lactic acid and nitrogen-rich urea, hormones and various proteins.

Red blood cells – 40–45%

You have around 25 billion red blood cells (erythrocytes) – 20 million in every 1mm³ (0.00006in³) of blood – and every one of them is packed with clever oxygen-binding haemoglobin. Your body produces 2.4 million new ones every day, each of them taking a week to build in your bone marrow before they get tidied up in your spleen. Red blood cells live for three to four months, travelling over 160km (100 miles) through your system and carrying oxygen from your lungs to your various tissues. Once they've become worn out by the brutal mechanics of circulation, their structure changes slightly and scavenger macrophage cells spot them and eat them.

White blood cells – 1%

Although they only make up 1% of your blood, white blood cells (leukocytes) are a vital part of your immune system (your body's main defence mechanism against invading organisms). They tirelessly patrol your highways and byways looking for pathogenic wrongdoers and fighting off their endless attacks, the vast majority of which you are totally unaware of. They come in two main varieties: eater (phagocytic) cells and non-eater (non-phagocytic) cells. **Lacking eyes and ears, eater cells are attracted to infections by chemical signals through a process called chemotaxis, and they can spot an astonishing 1 million different foreign proteins**.

Platelets – less than 1%

Platelets (thrombocytes) are blood-clotting tools that gather at the site of a rupture in a blood vessel and clump together, creating a temporary plug and kicking off a sequence of events called the 'coagulation cascade' that allows the body to patch and heal itself (see p34).

Bloodology

Although the oxygenated arterial blood that flows in the arteries deep inside your body is bright red, the carbon dioxide-rich venous blood that flows nearer the surface of your skin in your veins looks blue (take a look at your wrist and you should see). But annoyingly, it's not actually blue. Instead, your skin absorbs a lot of the long-wavelength red light that the blood reflects, leaving it looking blue on the surface.

Blood generally tastes rich and savoury (that comes from the proteins), with some sweetness from the glucose dissolved in it and a bit of saltiness from its various salts.

2.10 Scabs

Scabs are a crispy mixture of exudates ('stuff that oozes') made up of fibrin (a blood-clotting protein), pus-ey dead white blood cells and serum (blood plasma with all the clotting parts removed). They're a small, tasty and vital part of the fragile, complex and poorly understood wound-healing process. The body has a vast array of tools designed to stop the outside world from getting in, and cuts are a serious upset to these systems. That's why your **immune system throws a huge amount of effort into mending cuts and creating a barrier between you and your delightfully filthy, bug-infested environment**. The main stages of this process are clotting (whereby blood plugs the cut and begins to dry into a scab), inflammation, tissue growth and remodelling.

As soon as skin is cut, platelets gather and with the help of calcium, vitamin K and fibrinogen proteins, they begin to form a temporary plug to clot the blood and stop the flow. As fibrinogens sense air they break apart and form threads of fibrin that create a mesh to trap more blood cells, which eventually dries to form the scab covering that stops further bacteria from entering. Underneath this gloop, the battle against the invaders continues with microbe-eating white blood cells called macrophages eating bacterial cells until they run out of enzymes and die. A soup of millions of these is known as pus (see p24), which can sit tucked away under the scab for some time.

<u>Scabology</u>

I'm an enthusiastic scab-nibbler. It's not the taste that interests me (although they do have a meaty, protein-rich flavour), more important is the weird sense of achievement I get from eating them. It's not a good idea to pick your scabs, however, because you're letting in more bacteria, making your body vulnerable to the outside world and restarting the healing process. If it becomes a habit, it can also be seen as an obsessive-compulsive disorder similar to dermatophagia – biting and eating skin on your hands and fingers (which I must admit, I'm pretty keen on, too, see p120).

2.11 Sweat

You have around 2.5 million eccrine sweat glands* (see p137) all over your body. About half of them are on your back and chest, but your palms and the soles of your feet have the highest concentrations, with 600–700 sweat glands per cm² (0.16 sq in). **In the cold you produce about 535ml (18fl oz) of sweat a day** – women produce an average 420ml (14fl oz) and men an average 650ml (22fl oz) – but in hot weather and during exercise this can rise to an extraordinary 10–14 litres (18–25 pints) a day.

The sweat itself is a salty, acidic, odourless water containing tiny amounts of minerals, lactic acid and nitrogen-rich urea. You produce it to cool yourself down but this sweat-fountain is rare among mammals – horses are the only other ones to produce sweat on such a scale. The hotter you get, the faster the sweat flows and the more salty it is. This loss of salt can be dangerous as your body needs to maintain a specific level of saltiness.

To understand why sweat is so important you need to grasp the idea of homeostasis. This is your body's self-regulation system that keeps all the different bits of human machinery working at the right speed and at the right balance to keep you alive. This includes controlling lots of different mineral, salt and fluid levels, as well as blood acidity, blood pressure and body heat. This isn't just for comfort: hundreds of different chemical reactions are happening in your body right now and it's vital these take place at the right temperature because the warmer the environment, the faster the

*You also have a much smaller number of apocrine sweat glands that are found in more intimate places, such as the armpits, nipples, nose and genitalia.

Sweatology

Your body has an amazing ability to regulate its temperature and works tirelessly to keep you at 37°C (98.6°F), although a small variation of a degree or so at different times of the day is normal (your temperature is normally at its lowest two hours before you wake up). It also varies when you're ill but usually not by much – otherwise you're in serious trouble. For instance, a temperature of 40°C (104°F) is just a few degrees above normal but unless it drops quickly you'll have hyperthermia, which is life-threatening. A temperature of 41.5°C (106.7°F) or more is a serious medical emergency. Similarly, a drop of just a degree or two below normal (i.e. not just when you're sleeping) means hypothermia. Be careful out there.

chemical reaction. If your body is running too hot, these reactions happen too fast and you'll soon die. If you're running too cold, they happen too slowly and you'll soon die.

But exactly how does sweating cool us down? By a fantastic bit of physics called evaporative cooling. Your sweat glands secrete their salty water onto your skin, which then absorbs a surprising amount of body heat before becoming a vapour. This vapour then floats away, taking all that heat energy with it and leaving you cooler.

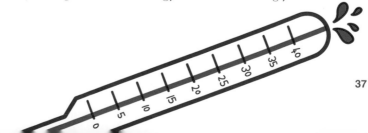

2.12 Tears

There are three different kinds of tears: basal tears are created constantly as a 'base' layer to keep the eyes moist and to protect their surface; reflex tears are activated to clean the eyes of foreign substances such as grit or smoke; while **emotional tears are psychogenic (they originate in the mind) and are a bit of a scientific mystery**.

The exact composition of your tears depends partly on which kind they are, but they all have a basic mix of ingredients that ooze from three types of gland. The lacrimal glands above the corners of your eyes furthest from your nose produce the main tear film – a clever protective watery solution containing salty electrolytes, antibodies, bacteria-killing lysozymes and lots more. The 50 or so meibomian glands along the rims of your eyelids produce meibum, an oily, waxy, protein-rich substance that stops the watery tear film from drying out. Lastly, your eye's goblet cells ooze slimy mucins that thicken the tears and spread them in a nice layer across the eyes. Interestingly, emotional tears seem to contain more protein-based hormones than basal or reflex tears but it's not clear why, and crying in general doesn't seem to have any evolutionary advantage.

Considering the vast amount of snot, sweat and spit you produce, you make a surprisingly small amount of tears – only 1ml (0.04fl oz) in a normal day (unless you've been crying) – which are spread by blinking. **You blink around 16,000 times a day (around 15–20 times a minute), with each blink lasting 100–400 milliseconds, but it's not clear why you do it so often**. You blink far more than you need just to keep your eyes moistened.

Reflexive blinking from loud noises or foreign bodies protects the eyes using the fastest muscle in the human body, a sphincter called the orbicularis oculi that makes your eyelids blink 4–7 million times every year.

Tearology

Why do onions make you cry? As your knife slices through an onion it cuts through thousands of cells that release enzymes as a defence mechanism. These break down and a chain of chemical reactions creates a liquid called syn-propanethial-S-oxide that rapidly evaporates into the air and, upon reaching your eyes, activates your lacrimal glands to produce lots of watery tears to wash it away. There are lots of 'cures' around to prevent this but most of them are totally useless. The only way of stopping yourself from crying is to chop onions underwater, though, of course, that also increases your chances of chopping a finger off.

2.13 Eye bogies

As a child, my mum used to tell me to rub the 'sleep' out of my eyes, which I always thought was an oddly poetic name for a bogey, even if it was one from my eyes. The substance itself is called rheum and in many ways it's similar to snot – it's a slippery, watery mucus produced by glands in the lining of the eyelids and the whites of the eye, but it also contains bacteria-fighting enzymes, immunoglobulins to identify viruses, as well as salts and glycoproteins. These are dissolved in water and held in a slimy gel by the mucins that we met in the section about snot (see p13). Rheum is fabulous stuff – it keeps your eyes moist and healthy, it helps to stop infections, and it traps any airborne microscopic particles of dust and bacteria that might land on your eyeballs.

When you're awake rheum is constantly produced but also constantly washed away from your eyes along with tears (and any nasties trapped in it) each time you blink. It all drains away into your nose through a tiny channel called the nasolacrimal duct ('naso' = nose, 'lacrimal' = tears) and gets added to the constant flow of snot moving through your nasal cavity. **Yes, some of your snot comes from your eyeballs!**

But why are eye bogies crispy and why do we only get them when we're asleep? Well, when you're asleep tear production slows down so the rheum isn't washed away. Some of it seeps out of your eyes, often into the corners of your eyelids, where it dries out into a nice light-coloured crispy blob. I am an enthusiastic nose bogey-eater (for health reasons, obvs) but I tend to pick and flick when it comes to eye bogies. I have tasted them, obviously, as a service to you, dear reader, but sadly they lack flavour other than a slight saltiness.

<u>Eye Bogeyology</u>

Eye bogies are only a problem when you have a lot
more than normal, when they get caught in your
eyelashes (rather than at the corner of your eyelids),
or when they have an unusual colour. The latter might
mean that there's pus mixed in, and when rheum
contains pus it's a whole different thing with a whole
new name: mucopurulent discharge. It's often a sign
that you have conjunctivitis, a common infection
that can make your eyes pink, inflamed and itchy.
Sometimes there's so much discharge that your eye is
glued shut when you wake up in the morning, which
feels really weird, although applying warm water
usually sorts it out.

2.14 Toe cheese

Feet are covered in lots of sweat glands that ooze into your socks, creating a tightly wrapped, warm, damp, salty, dark environment – pretty much the dream combination for the rapid growth of bacteria. Hence the stinking mixture of fetid bacteria and dead skin cells that, if you're lucky enough to have other fungal issues too, can be scraped like Boursin from between your toes using a firm fingernail. This is toe cheese, or toe jam if you prefer, and as well as dead skin and millions of bacteria and fungi, it also contains oils, sweat residue and sock fluff.

The medical term for smelly feet is bromodosis, and it's most common in teenagers and pregnant women, who are both likely to be experiencing hormonal changes that encourage sweating. The good news is that it's unlikely to be bad for you, although if you have broken skin, it can upgrade to a bacterial infection.

Most microbes that live on the skin are not harmful to us – indeed many are beneficial – but the smell comes from organic acids as well as the (notoriously putrid) sulphur-based thiols that the microbes produce as by-products. There are many different flavour volatiles at play here, but **the cheesy smell often comes from isovaleric acid (found in Swiss cheese), as well as certain bacteria that feet and fine cheese share**. Different bacteria prefer different parts of the body, and the ones that like your toes are mostly corynebacteria, micrococcineae and staphylococcaceae (which all enjoy your slightly acidic foot sweat). These are joined by a variety of yeasts and dermatophyte fungi. There are around 60 species of fungi in your toenails, 40 between your toes and a whopping 80 on your heels.

2.15 Tongue cheese

Tongue cheese is the slurry on your tongue that you can collect if you rake it hard enough with your front teeth or employ a scraper. It's a mixture of saliva, dead cells, food and drink residues, and bacteria and bacterial waste that enjoy the dark, damp, wet, conditions in your mouth. **Everyone has a version of this stuff, and it's unlikely to be harmful, but there's decent evidence that tongue scraping can be useful, especially if you suffer from halitosis** (bad breath, see p142). A Belgian study showed that scraping improves your sense of taste; an American study found that it reduces bacteria known to cause tooth decay and halitosis; and a 2004 study published in the *Journal of Periodontology* concluded that a tongue scraper was better than a toothbrush at tackling the volatile sulphur compounds often responsible for bad breath.

Chapter 03:
Rude Noises

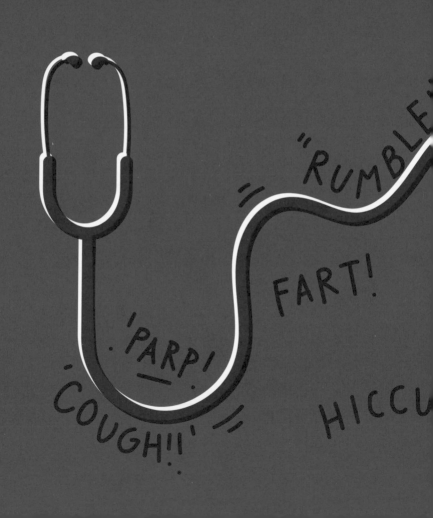

3.01 Your noisy body

There's a lot you can learn from auscultation, the technique of listening to the body with a stethoscope (a device invented by Frenchman René Laennec in 1816 – his first version was beautifully simple: a rolled-up piece of paper). The main organs that medics like to listen to are the ones in constant motion: the lungs (which never stop respiring), the heart (which never stops pumping blood) and the digestive tract (which never stops churning food by peristalsis – and various other squeezes and squirts).

BURP!!

HA!

CHOO!

SNIFF!

CRACK!

3.02 Burps

Burps are small but socially reviled releases of gas from the stomach and oesophagus. Lots of mammals burp, especially ruminants such as cows and sheep, which emit vast amounts of methane, among other gases. **The Guinness World Record for the loudest burp is 112.4 decibels, set by Neville Sharp in Darwin, Australia, on 29 July 2021**. Well done, Neville.

Burps are usually caused by swallowing air when eating or drinking, or by consuming fizzy drinks that contain lots of dissolved carbon dioxide, some of which only turns into gas after it's swallowed. As gases build up in the stomach they float upwards and press against the gastro-oesophageal sphincter – the tap at the top of your stomach. Eventually this opens just enough to release a squirt of air that vibrates both the throat and the sphincter itself, just like a fart (see p52)! Indigestion tablets called antacids can make you burp – they often contain alkaline calcium carbonate, which reacts with your acidic gastric juices, and the resulting acid-base reaction produces carbon dioxide gas. Chewing gum can cause you to swallow more air than normal, and this is also likely to result in more burping.

Burping is, like farting, one of those perfectly normal mechanisms that has for some bizarre reason come to be seen as rude. Heaven knows why – burping is essential for humans to be able to release intestinal pressure that would otherwise become uncomfortable or dangerous.

<u>Burpology</u>

A small number of people are unable to burp, and they can suffer from abdominal pain and bloating. Young babies often suffer from abdominal pain after swallowing too much air while feeding, and happy is the parent who has nailed their burping technique, because a gassy baby is a loud, screaming baby.

It is possible to burp and hiccup at the same time but it can be painful. When the hiccup's diaphragm spasm pulls air into the lungs at the same time as the burp makes its way up the oesophagus, there's a sharp increase in pressure on the glottis and vocal cords that can really hurt. Avoid.

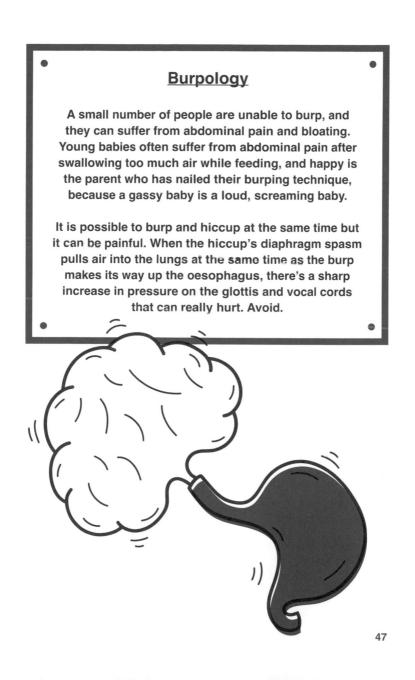

3.03 Hiccups

What's the evolutionary point of hiccups? Nobody knows. They offer us no physiological advantage whatsoever, which is strange considering that we all experience them. They are easily triggered by fizzy drinks, eating too fast, or eating too much, and babies even hiccup in the womb. I get them after eating an unexpectedly spicy mouthful of food.

Hiccups (more formally known as singultus) are an example of an autonomic reflex arc: an involuntary sequence of events that occurs without your brain having to process the information about them. These automatic responses happen quickly, and include the withdrawal reflex – when you jerk your hand away after touching something hot. The downside is you have little or no control over them, which is why your hiccups are so hard to stop.

The mechanics of hiccups are simple: once the action is triggered, a fast, involuntary contraction of the diaphragm opens up the lungs and draws in air. Then, 35 milliseconds later, the vocal cords close, stopping the flow of air and making the 'hup' sound we know so well. At the same time, you experience a twitch or tremor involving a part of your upper body – usually the shoulders, abdomen and/or throat.

Among the more interesting theories about the evolutionary advantage of hiccups is the burping reflex hypothesis, a relatively solid theory published in *BioEssays* in 2012. The idea is that hiccups are a tool to help suckling babies drink as much milk as possible. Air in the stomach swallowed when drinking takes up valuable space, so the air triggers the hiccup, which creates low pressure in the throat and causes the burp to be sucked out of the stomach. Adult hiccups

are simply an echo of this infantile reflex. But as the author of the theory admits, 'There is, as yet, no proof for this hypothesis…'. There's another theory that hiccups are related to tadpole breathing mechanics but that all feels a bit hopeful.

Treatments for hiccups vary from hocus-pocus folk cures to pretty serious invasive surgery for 'intractable hiccups' – those that last longer than a month. **One interesting cure that's been successful in several clinical cases is digital rectal massage, otherwise known as 'wiggling a finger up your bum'.** Weren't expecting that, were you?

Hiccupology

The worst recorded case of hiccups is attributed to American Charles Osbourne, who hiccupped for 68 years, doing so an estimated 430 million times. The hiccups began when he tried to lift a very heavy pig and ended – for no apparent reason – in February 1990, a year before he died. Bummer, huh?

3.04 Sneezes

Sneezing, also known as sternutation, is semi-autonomous: you only have partial control of it, like blinking and breathing. It's a violent expulsion of air through your nose and mouth designed to clear foreign particles, usually in reaction to something physically or chemically irritating your nasal mucosa. Other possible stimuli include breathing cold air, eating apples, illness, overeating, sexual arousal and looking into a light*.

As you sneeze, mechanisms in the throat change shape to create a vacuum effect at the back of the nose, sucking stray juices out while dislodging some of the surface mucus. These juices can easily create 40,000 droplets of mucus, saliva, and assorted aerosolized bits and bobs.

The impulse to sneeze is triggered when microbes or debris get past your nose hairs and reach the nasal mucosa, triggering the release of histamines that irritate underlying nerve cells and then send a signal to the brain that leads to the sneeze. **The sneeze plume can travel as far as 8m (26ft)**, and any infectious aerosol droplets easily spread disease.

*This was first discovered in the 1950s by a French researcher who realized that some of his patients sneezed when he shined his ophthalmoscope into their eyes. This became known as a photic sneeze reflex, and although it's been well studied (odd for a condition that isn't particularly dangerous), no one really knows why it happens.

<u>Sneezology</u>

You usually can't sneeze in your sleep because your body enters a state of rapid eye movement-associated atonia: a remarkable and almost complete paralysis under which motor neurons (that control muscles and glands) become hyperpolarized so that it takes a much stronger stimulus to excite them.

When you're awake it's not a good idea to hold a sneeze in as it can create high pressures in the respiratory system that can rupture body tissue. Sneezes feel good partly because your body releases endorphins afterwards and partly because any release of pressure in the body feels good.

3.05 Flatus

You produce around 1.5 litres (2.6 pints) of gas a day in 10–15 separate farts, created mainly by the 39–100 trillion microbes that live in your gut. If that sounds like a lot of guff, remember that many of these can pop out during your sleep or when you go to the toilet. Lots of people are embarrassed by farts and even I have to admit there's a time and a place for them. But they are also an essential part of our digestive system, so it seems odd they make us so uptight. **If you didn't fart, you'd explode** – well, strictly speaking, a few other revolting things would happen first, including the gas being forced to travel the wrong way through your digestive system, causing you unbearable pain, before farting out through your mouth. No one wants that, so on balance, it's best to love your farts. I love them so much that I wrote *Fartology*, an entire book about the extraordinary chemistry, physics and biology behind them.

Flatus is 25% swallowed air mixed with gases from your body that have diffused back into your digestive system. The other 75% is made in your gut itself: a combination of carbon dioxide, hydrogen, nitrogen, occasionally methane, plus a tiny amount of flavour volatiles that give your fart its unique smell. Generally speaking, fibrous foods (mainly fruits and vegetables) broken down by bacteria in the colon are responsible for the volume of your farts, while proteins (eggs, meat, fish, beans, nuts), which are mainly broken down by enzymes in your small intestine, are responsible for their smell.

Not all farts are made the same. Women's farts often pack a stronger punch. Although men create more gas than women overall, a 1998 study published in the academic journal *Gut* found that women's farts tend to be smellier. This is because their microbiome (see p123) is more likely to contain bacteria that produce eggy hydrogen sulphide as they break food down. Women's guts are also likely to contain more methane-producing methanobacteria, meaning 60% of women produce methane compared with just 40% of men. As a result women's farts are also more flammable.

One of the flavour volatiles found in smellier farts is the powerful thiol methanethiol, which energy companies add to household gas to help warn you of a gas leak. Methane is scarily odourless, making it difficult to know if your gas supply is leaking, but the added methanethiol is so putrid that you can smell it at surprisingly low concentrations. When the gas burns properly the methanethiol is destroyed and there's no smell but, still, I love the fact that your gas company is effectively farting into your house.

Why are some farts hotter than others?

It's all down to the metabolic process: the series of chemical changes in the cells of organic matter that convert fuel for your body to use and build new components. When bacteria convert fuel by glycolysis, glucose is catabolized (broken down) into pyruvate, which is then broken down further, and this reaction releases lots of heat – hence hot farts.

You tend to get hot stinky farts when conditions are perfect for the turbocharged metabolism of food: that is, when there's loads of fuel available to your gut bacteria (i.e. you've eaten lots of dietary fibre); when your gut is super-populated with active bacteria, either because it's been well-fed with fibre over a long period of time, or because you've eaten lots of probiotics; and when your gut is at optimal operating conditions, for example, when internal heat and levels of acidity are perfect. In this case both fart volume and smell should be at extremely high levels. Settle in and enjoy the ride.

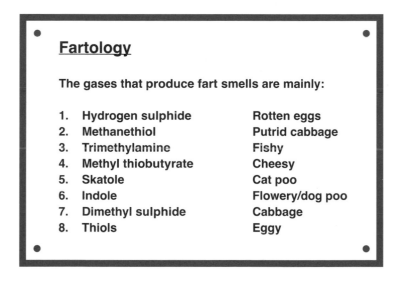

Fartology

The gases that produce fart smells are mainly:

1. **Hydrogen sulphide** — **Rotten eggs**
2. **Methanethiol** — **Putrid cabbage**
3. **Trimethylamine** — **Fishy**
4. **Methyl thiobutyrate** — **Cheesy**
5. **Skatole** — **Cat poo**
6. **Indole** — **Flowery/dog poo**
7. **Dimethyl sulphide** — **Cabbage**
8. **Thiols** — **Eggy**

Fart acoustics

Sound comes from vibrations that create sequences of pressure waves. Humans can only hear these pressure waves if their frequency is between 20 times per second in the case of low bass sounds (20Hz) and 20,000 times per second in the case of high treble sounds (20KHz). So, farts must generate a vibration within that range to be heard. That generator is your anus – specifically the external opening of the rectum, tightly controlled by two sets of circular muscles known as the inner sphincter and the outer sphincter.

As fart gases build up in your rectum (the storage tank for gas and poo), the **pressure increases, which you feel as a need to fart or poo because a clever set of tiny mechanoreceptors send messages to your brain saying so (they can even tell the difference between a fart and a poo)**. When you decide to relax your outer sphincter (you have no control over the inner sphincter), the pressurized gas is able to push open a small hole through your anus.

But why does your anus vibrate when you release a fart, causing that all-important raspberry sound? Well, it's all about pressure and friction. The sphincter opens just a crack to let the fart out, but as soon as the gas is moving it sucks the anal sphincter back together as the fart flows through it. This is partly because a faster flow creates lower pressure, partly because the fart curves around the edge of the sphincter as it goes, and partly because, as soon as the hole opens, the pressure drops ever so slightly in your rectum. This closes the hole momentarily, but almost as soon as it closes, the pressure builds up a little more, pushing the hole open again, which then lowers the pressure to shut it again. This then repeats over and over until the pressure drops completely. As long as that opening and closing happens at least 20 times a second – bingo! You've created a series of pressure waves within the audible range and you have a fart.

You can also change the sound of your farts by tightening or loosening your sphincter as the fart flows out – the tighter you squeeze, the higher the note should be as you increase the pressure of the gas in your rectum, and the faster it vibrates due to the tighter sphincter and smaller hole.

EXPERIMENT 2

HOW TO CATCH YOUR FARTS IN A JAR
It's very easy to catch your farts in a jar should you
wish to isolate them for closer investigation, or just
for sh*ts and giggles. Run a bath without adding any
salts or bubbly soaps that might interfere with the
flavours, then submerge yourself in it along with your
jar. Lower the jar entirely underwater and let it fill with
water, then place it, upside down, above your anus.
Let rip, and you'll find that the gas floats up and
displaces a volume of water equal to its own volume
(thanks to Archimedes' physical law of buoyancy)
and you can secure the lid. Turn the jar upside down
and Bob's your fart, floating atop the remaining water.
A word of caution: don't wait too long before using
the fart because those flavour volatiles are, as you'd
imagine, volatile. They likely won't stick around intact
for long before oxidizing or reacting with other gases
and the water, losing their special powers.

3.06 Coughing

Acough is a clever bit of fluid dynamics designed to clear the airways of phlegm, irritants and foreign particles, and it follows a clear sequence. First, there's a deep inhalation of air into the lungs. Then the glottis (the opening between the vocal cords) closes, snapping the vocal cords shut. The diaphragm relaxes and the abdomen tenses, forcing the lungs to build up air pressure against the vocal cords, and finally the glottis opens again, allowing a violent expulsion of air that can carry unwanted substances out of the throat (and preferably into a waiting tissue).

Is it bad to cough? Well, that airflow can be pretty destructive, and it doesn't take many coughs before your delicate throat tissues become inflamed and sore. Coughing also forces droplets of phlegm and saliva bearing microbes to aerosolize and travel a surprising distance through the air, spreading viruses and bacteria to others. While coughing is useful for clearing the airways, it can also be a sign of respiratory tract infection, such as flu, bronchitis, COVID-19 or tuberculosis.

Another type of cough is the flimsily understood psychogenic or tic cough, also known as somatic cough syndrome. **Many people cough out of habit rather than for medical reasons but it isn't well understood why.** Somatization refers to the transfer of psychological distress into a physical symptom but there's little consensus on causes or diagnosis.

Coughology

Despite the amount of cough medicines available, there are surprisingly few evidence-based solutions for coughs. The effectiveness of cough medicines seems to be minimal and, in the USA and Canada, they aren't recommended for children aged six and under. A 2014 review by medical research charity Cochrane concluded: 'There is no good evidence for or against the effectiveness of OTC (over the counter) medicines in acute cough'. The NHS clearly says that cough syrup, medicine and sweets 'will not stop your cough' and that 'decongestants and cough medicines containing codeine will not stop your cough'. Nonetheless more than £500m is spent each year on OTC treatments for cough and cold medicines in the UK alone. Of course, we all want to stop our coughs and help our loved ones to feel better, and are willing to throw money at the problem, but bear in mind that 90% of children's coughs disappear without treatment after 25 days. Just saying.

3.07 Laughing

The study of laughter is called gelotology. Laughter is one of the few universal human communication tools common to all languages and ages. **You begin to laugh at 15–17 weeks and even children born deaf and blind are able to laugh**. Whereas species such as chimpanzees, gorillas and orangutans laugh in response to physical stimuli such as tickling, play-fighting and play-chasing, humans are the only animals that experience emotional laughter, which has no physical stimulus. Rats have an ultrasonic play-and-tickle laugh (they also use this laugh during mating), dogs have a play-pant, and dolphins make a pulse-whistle combination during play-fighting. A hyena's laugh doesn't count either way – it's an expression of fear, excitement or frustration.

Humans also laugh in response to joy and embarrassment, relief, funny stories or concepts, in response to drugs such as alcohol and nitrous oxide, and even as a mechanism for coping with anger, frustration or sadness. But perhaps most importantly humans laugh as a form of social bonding. Research shows that **you are 30 times more likely to laugh in the company of others than when you're alone**. You also develop a fake laugh to use in polite situations as an agreement, acknowledgement or simply to indicate that you've heard or understood what another person has said.

As with crying (see p156), the significance of laughter and its neural mechanism isn't well understood. That said, we do know that laughing prompts us to produce endorphins that can reduce pain and make us feel good, and at the same time suppresses stress hormones such as epinephrine and cortisol.

Laughology

The physical experience of laughter is oddly dramatic, hijacking vital functions such as breathing, heart rate and pulse, as well as forcing rhythmic convulsions of the diaphragm and vocal cords. You can't breathe properly while laughing and no doubt an alien watching you laugh would be seriously worried about your health. There have been a few rare stories of people laughing themselves to death including that of Alex Mitchell from King's Lynn, who died while watching the 'Kung Fu Kapers' episode of *The Goodies* comedy show in 1975. He laughed continuously for 25 minutes and then passed away from heart failure. His widow later sent a letter to the team behind *The Goodies* thanking them for making Mitchell's final moments so pleasant.

3.08 Knuckle cracks

know all about crepitus, the term for popping and cracking joints, because my daughter Poppy is a demon knuckle-cracker. It's all about cavitation: the formation and then collapse of tiny bubbles of gas in our joints.

The main crackable joints are those at the base of our fingers known as the third metacarpophalangeal (MCP) joints. The bones in these MCP joints squeeze together and pull apart all the time, changing the pressure in the synovial fluid that sits inside the joint for lubrication. When this movement makes the pressure in the fluid drop, little bubbles can form. The same thing happens in a bottle of fizzy drink – before you open it, the liquid is under pressure, and at that pressure, the carbon dioxide (CO_2) gas inside it is happily dissolved in the drink, but when you unscrew the lid, the pressure drops and some of the CO_2 evaporates from the liquid, expanding and becoming bubbles of gas.

So now you have little bubbles floating in the synovial fluid in your joints. Next comes the exciting bit. If you bend your knuckles back, you build up pressure in that same fluid, and as it increases, the little bubbles are put back under pressure. They're ready to collapse and condense back into a liquid, but this doesn't happen slowly and gently – **some bubbles collapse very fast, releasing a large amount of energy and generating a shock wave. That audible shock wave is the knuckle crack**.

Some people can't crack their knuckles, which is thought to be because they have larger spaces and hence more synovial fluid between their bones. The more fluid there is, the harder it is to create a pressure change big enough for bubbles to form and collapse.

EXPERIMENT 3

SHOCK WAVE IN A CAN
How does a little condensing gas in the knuckle create a shock wave? Here's an excellent and simple demonstration of the physics behind it*. Gather an empty aluminium drinks can, a large bowl full of cold water, a pair of heatproof tongs and either a gas hob or a gas camping stove. Give the can a quick rinse and tip most of the water out, leaving a few drops inside. Place the large bowl of water on a solid surface next to the hob or gas burner, and light the gas. Turn the can upside down and pick it up firmly with the tongs. Hold it, with the open side pointing down, over the flame for 10 seconds or so until you can see a little steam coming out of it, then slowly and carefully lower the very hot can (still upside down and held vertically) into the water. The steam inside the can will condense extremely fast, and the can will implode and crumple with a sharp 'crack'. That's the phase change from gas to liquid happening, and it's surprisingly noisy. Suddenly the knuckle crack makes a lot of sense.

*If you're a (ridiculously cool) child (and I know these books appeal to kids as well as adults), get one of those old people to help you do this as there's a danger of burns.

3.09 Stomach rumbles

Your guts are basically one fascinating, unceasingly active 4-m (13-ft) long* tube that churns and pushes food through your body from mouth to sphincter, mainly using peristalsis, a sequence of muscle contractions that pushes the food along like toothpaste in a tube.

A rumbling stomach (known as borborygmus) isn't caused by the movement of food itself, but by gases interacting with food and drink when peristalsis squeezes sections of the stomach and small intestine squirting the mixture through them. These gases are a combination of swallowed air and gases created by the metabolic process. In your small intestine carbon dioxide is often produced when sodium bicarbonate neutralizes acids from the stomach, whereas in your large intestine the gases are by-products of bacteria breaking down fibrous food.

The glugging, squelching noises are perfectly normal, if a little disconcerting. **The only time to worry is when the noises are different to normal or stop altogether**. A doctor can listen to the sounds using a stethoscope but will probably be more interested in hearing a lack of sound, which might mean you have an intestinal obstruction or your normal peristaltic motion isn't working, both of which are very serious indeed. If your stomach rumbles really bother you, you can quieten them to some extent by eating more slowly, thus swallowing less air, and by avoiding fizzy drinks and chewing gum.

*The digestive tract is somewhere between 2.7m and 5m (9ft and 16ft) long, although estimates of length vary enormously. This is partly because living human guts are almost constantly contracting, so are shorter than those in the dead bodies used for medical research, which are relaxed and therefore longer.

3.10 Snoring

Snoring is a widespread phenomenon that affects 57% of adult men and 40% of adult women – and every single mammal in my house, including the hamster. **The world record for loudest snoring is held by Kåre Walkert for peak levels of 93 decibels while asleep** at Sweden's Örebro Regional Hospital on 24 May 1993. Snoring is an interesting phenomenon and it's caused by a relaxation of the uvula* and the soft palate high up at the back of your mouth, combined with a relaxation of the throat. This causes throat tissues to block the airway enough to create turbulence and vibration, just like a flag flapping in the wind. The greater the blockage, the louder the snore.

Other than your own natural mouth anatomy, snoring can be caused by allergies, weight gain, drinking alcohol, nasal congestion, sedatives and irregular sleeping positions (especially sleeping on your back), and also by sleep deprivation, which is both a cause and a symptom. Other serious symptoms include behavioural problems, aggression and frustration, lack of concentration, and a greater risk of high blood pressure, stroke and heart conditions.

Obstructive sleep apnea (OSA) is often associated with snoring but is a more serious condition that causes repeated breath failures during sleep and tends to sound a lot more dramatic, as though a person is choking or gasping for air. It can cause a wide variety of problems, from high blood pressure to metabolic dysfunction, obesity and depression, so if you suffer from really bad snoring, it's a good idea to check in with your doctor.

*That weird dangly thing at the back of your throat, properly known as the palatine uvula, used to close off your nasopharynx and stop food entering the nasal cavity.

3.11 Sighing

The sigh is a versatile tool for expressing a vast range of negativity, from light parental disappointment to deep relationship-related melancholy. Sighing can be a reaction to stress and anxiety but you also do it constantly throughout the day without realizing it, and for an oddly positive reason. **These automatic 'basal sighs' happen every five minutes or so, and are seen in many other mammals, too**.

A fascinating study by researchers at UCLA and Stanford found that sighing is a vital reflex action that helps preserve lung function. You have 500 million tiny, balloon-like alveoli in your lungs that open and close throughout the day to take in air and exchange carbon dioxide in your blood for oxygen. But occasionally some of these alveoli collapse. By making you inhale twice as much air as normal, a good sigh puts pressure on them to re-inflate. It's a little like blowing into a crushed fizzy drinks bottle to return it to its original shape. This might sound like a minor problem but genetically engineered mice unable to sigh eventually die of major lung problems.

The medical definition of a sigh is a deep augmented breath followed by a pause, known as a post-sigh apnea. Sighs can stabilize and reset breathing variability after exercise, speaking or sleeping. **Too much sighing can lead to panic attacks and too little sighing is associated with SIDS (Sudden Infant Death Syndrome)**.

In addition to its physiological function, sighing can be a stress-response, a reaction to anxiety, negativity and tiredness. But Professor Jack Feldman, one of the UCLA/Stanford team, says we don't know why this is: 'There is certainly a component of sighing that relates to an emotional state. When you are stressed, for example, you sigh more. It may be that neurons in the brain areas that process emotion are triggering the release of the sigh neuropeptides – but we don't know that.'

Chapter 04:
Revolting Skin

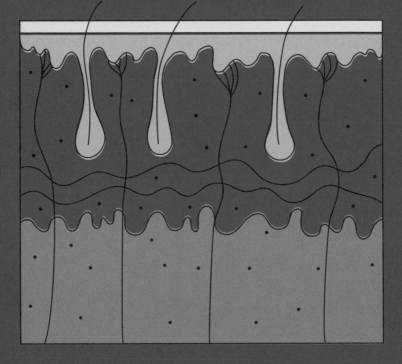

4.01 Skin science

I t's often said that the skin is the largest organ in the human body, with a surface area of about 1.8m^2 (19 sq ft). That doesn't quite hold true because the surface area of the small intestine alone is at least 15 times larger and there's even some debate about whether the interstitium* is larger. By weight, skin's the big-hitter at over 6kg (13lb), easily beating the next-heaviest, the intestines at 3.5kg (7.7lb). But let's stop this organ-swinging nonsense – it doesn't matter, because skin is extraordinary.

Your skin is made of multiple layers (up to seven, depending on what you count as a layer) and there are two overall types: hairy skin and glabrous hairless skin. Although humans are the least hairy primates, the vast majority of your skin is the hairy type and your only bits of glabrous skin are on your lips, fingers, palms, nipples, soles of your feet, and parts of the genitals (both male and female).

The thickness of your skin varies between 0.3mm (0.01in) on your elbows and 4mm (0.15in) on the soles of your feet. It is also in a constant state of renewal due to the cycle of skin cell division deep in the epidermis. As skin cells divide and multiply they are pushed slowly towards the surface, replacing the old ones as they go, and eventually dying themselves, filling with tough keratin (when they're known as squames, or scales) and finally rubbing off or flaking away. You might like the look of yourself in the mirror but what you're seeing is dead human: the outermost layer of your skin

*The interstitium is the network of flexible, fluid-filled connective tissue spaces found throughout your body and your main source of lymph fluid. It's also a protective layer a little like a car's suspension system, absorbing the flexing and bulging of your body's organs as they go about their work.

(the stratum corneum) is all lifeless cells. Between 500 to 3,000 cells exfoliate from every 1cm² (0.16 sq in) of skin per hour, which means **you lose up to 600,000 to a million or more dead skin cells every 60 minutes**. You replace your entire epidermis every 30 days and in the process create about 500g (1lb) of human dust each year.

Skin has many functions: it protects our internal mechanics from the daily onslaught of knocks, scratches and invading microbial hordes, but it's also our environmental interface, a porous, water-resistant (but not waterproof) border between us and the world. Semi-permeable like an eggshell, it oozes liquids such as sweat through various glands but allows oxygen in by absorption (and nanoparticles less than 40nm in diameter can penetrate it). This is essential as your outer layers of skin have no capillaries to feed them oxygenated blood, so they have no choice but to get their oxygen from the atmosphere.

Skinology

House dust can comprise 20–50% dead skin cells.

Some tattoos have magnetic inks in their pigments, so if you have an MRI scan (during which you lie inside a vast, enormously powerful magnet), your tattoo can tingle or even burn, though this is very rare.

Your skin hosts nearly 1 billion bacteria per 1cm² (0.16 sq in) – or 1.6 trillion across an average 1.8m² (19 sq ft) human.

The Guinness World Record for the stretchiest skin belongs to Garry Turner, who can stretch the skin on his abdomen 15.9cm (6.3in) and pull the skin on his neck up over his mouth and nose like a snood. Yet despite this, he's remarkably wrinkle-free. He suffers from a rare genetic disorder called Ehlers-Danlos syndrome that can severely weaken skin, blood vessels and joints. It affects collagen fibres in about one in 500,000 people, making them 'disorderly' and causing skin to feel thin and stretchy. Garry gets cuts and grazes more easily than most people, and suffers extreme pain in his joints.

4.02 Zits

Ah, how unfondly I remember my teenage snog-blockers. Zits come in three main forms: nice tight blackheads, scarily pustulous whiteheads and annoying red lumps that may or may not turn into a blackhead or whitehead, depending on whether the God of Acne is smiling or frowning upon you that day. Anyone who's visited the doctor about their zits knows there's no simple solution to them. The only useful advice is also the most utterly useless advice: 'Don't squeeze them'. We all know it, and we all squeeze them anyway. That's just the way life works.

Zits are characteristic features of acne vulgaris, an annoying, long-term and common skin condition that primarily affects teenagers (especially teenage boys) – but also a vital tool for helping adults feel less depressed that their best days have already passed them by. **Acne is so common that 80% of people will suffer from it at some point in their lives**. But the name only refers to the chronic inflammatory condition, not to simply discovering a single juicy rice pop-style smasher the very evening you're heading out on a date with The One.

Blackheads

The formal name for a blackhead is an open comedo and the mechanism behind one is simple. Oily sebum constantly oozes into our hair follicles to keep our hair luxuriantly glossy. At the same time, the linings of these follicles are continuously shed. The lining debris and the sebum usually escape to the surface of our skin and get wiped away by bodily movements, but sometimes they get trapped. When this happens, sebum builds up in the follicle while the skin-cell debris turns black as the melanin oxidizes. This plugs the pore, creating the blackhead. It's known as an 'open' comedo because there's no layer of living skin above the plug. The dead cells trapped underneath can create bacterial infection, usually involving *Staphylococcus aureus* and *Cutibacterium acnes*. On the plus side, blackheads generally squeeze up a treat (which, of course, you shouldn't do).

Whiteheads

Known fondly as a 'milk hotel' or 'pimplestiltskin', the closed comedo differs from the 'open' variety by having a covering of skin rather than a plug. When the trapped debris gets infected with bacteria, white blood cells arrive to kill them and as these metabolize the bacteria, they die and turn into pus. Again, whiteheads squeeze up a treat (which, of course, you shouldn't do).

You shouldn't squeeze your zits because each time you do, you create a small opening in the skin that can get reinfected with the pustulous, bacteria-infected goo you've just squeezed out. Such infections can be dangerous and are more likely to result in scarring. If you leave zits to their own devices, they will invariably go away of their own accord. Excellent advice which, of course, you are going to ignore, so I don't know why I'm bothering to tell you.

4.03 Boils & carbuncles

I t's tempting to think of boils as rocket-powered mega-zits but the truth is both deeper and more dangerous. The medical term for them is furuncles and though they're similar to zits, they are rooted deeper beneath the skin and are much more painful infections of the hair follicle. They are also potentially life-threatening. The thing about boils is that they really, REALLY hurt. Unlike zits, they are usually caused by *Streptococcus pyogenes* or particularly nasty *Staphylococcus aureus* bacteria that have multiplied deep in the skin and been attacked by white blood cells called macrophages (see p26), which consume them. After eating several bacteria, each white blood cell exhausts its supply of enzymes and dies. Together with other phagocytized (eaten) cells, undestroyed bacteria and dead tissue, they make up the yellowish soup we know as pus (see p24), and as this accumulates under the inflamed skin it becomes even more painful. I have terrifying memories from when I was around four of my mum trying to squeeze a boil on my bum while I lay over a bean bag, screaming in a combination of humiliation and agony.

If you're unlucky enough to have a cluster of several boils, it's known as a carbuncle. **Both boils and carbuncles can grow to the size of golf balls**. They can also grow close to your eye, in which case they are called styes. The bacteria found inside boils are infectious and can easily spread to other people. They can also turn nasty, even life-threatening, if they get into your bloodstream. Never squeeze a boil around your nose or mouth in case the infection enters adjacent blood vessels that supply the brain, which can be particularly nasty.

<u>Boilology</u>

So what do you do when you have a boil that looks ready to pop? First, DO NOT BURST IT, for the reasons I've just mentioned (which I wish someone had mentioned to my mum). The dangers of reinfection and contagion are serious, so head to the doctor straight away to get it checked and, most likely, lanced. Your doc may offer you antibiotics but one of the annoying things about *Staphylococcus aureus* is its ability to develop antibiotic resistance, so don't be surprised if you're just told to keep it clean and dressed.

4.04 Jock rot

A fruity name for a fruity problem. An itchy groin is never a barrel of laughs, and jock rot, formally known as tinea cruris, is no exception. **It's a red, itchy, embarrassing, contagious fungal infection of the groin**, and is often suffered by men who are also affected by athlete's foot, fungal nail infection and problematic sweating. Different fungi are to blame across the world but antifungal medication usually treats it effectively. If you're prone to it, try wearing looser-fitting clothing and keeping your groin nice and dry – fungal infections thrive in warm, dark, moist environments.

Needless to say, it's best to keep your fungi to yourself and avoid rubbing your groin against anyone else's until they've all packed their suitcases and buggered off.

4.05 Moles

M oles are formally known as naevi (the singular is naevus) and they are very common skin lesions. Most people have 10–40 of them scattered all over their body. They come in all shapes, sizes and colours (the word naevi covers a huge variety of different lesions and bumps), and they can come and go, or change their appearance for no good reason. **Black-, pink-, red- or even blue-coloured naevi aren't unusual**.

The vast majority are completely harmless (but dramatic-sounding) melanocytic tumours. These benign tumours are clusters of melanocyte melanin pigment-producing cells that malfunction to produce a local overgrowth of dark pigmented cells. I have a corker of a hairy mole on my belly, and I can't work out whether I love it or hate it.

Very occasionally moles can become cancerous, and the main signs for spotting these are change and unevenness. If you have a mole that doesn't have a clear border, is unevenly coloured, made of more than one colour, gets bigger, or starts itching, flaking or bleeding, it's best to get it looked at by a doctor.

Moleology

There's no strict definition of a beauty spot, although they are usually melanocytic tumours – similar to my vast belly mole, which is the size of an actual blind subterranean mammal. In several eras it has been fashionable to apply artificial ones, either using make-up or a small patch known as a mouche (from the French for 'fly'). Mouches could also be used to hide syphilis sores (often found adjacent to the mouth) and smallpox scars. For my money, the most famous beauty spot was Marilyn Monroe's but Dolly Parton's is up there, too.

4.06 Birthmarks

Skin irregularities come in such a variety of forms that calling one a mole and another a birthmark is sometimes pointless. Neither word has a strict definition, but there's an undeniable romance attached to the idea of a birthmark. The birthmark on my foot is coloured, very much under the skin, doesn't protrude, looks like a small bruise, isn't a worry, and provides me with some badly needed physical quirkiness. Yours are probably different and cooler.

Birthmarks come in two main varieties: pigmented (coloured) and vascular (related to blood vessels). Pigmented birthmarks include the Mongolian spot, a common blue-ish colouring under the skin that looks a little like a bruise and usually disappears before puberty. **The delightfully named *café au lait* spot is a flat, light-brown colouration that has lots of possible causes**. And of course, you can also dub any old mole a birthmark should you wish to endow your bits with some added romance.

Vascular birthmarks include beautiful raised 'strawberry marks' (also known as infantile hemangiomas), which protrude a little and tend to disappear within a few years. There are also 'stork bites', which many babies are born with. These are areas of skin in which the capillaries (tiny blood vessels) are a little wider than normal, giving a red, inflamed appearance, and they usually disappear before the age of two.

Some birthmarks can be removed using surgical lasers, steroids or surgery. But it seems a shame to take away something that's a mark of your individuality. We should learn to love birthmarks and those who have them – though I know that life, society and mean people can make it a bit more complicated than that.

4.07 Bunions

No one knows the exact cause of bunions, also known as hallux valgus. They're a deformity of the big-toe joint that gives the foot a strange diamond shape – the joint points outwards away from the other toes, spreading out the front of the foot, while the front section of the toe points inwards. To the uneducated eye, they look like a symptom of wearing tight high-heeled shoes, and they certainly affect women more than men. An extraordinary 23% of adults suffer from bunions and **researchers have found extensive evidence of them in English skeletons from the 14th and 15th centuries, a period that coincided with a fashion for pointy shoes**.

Bunions can be painful, and even require surgery, so it's not big or clever to mock sufferers by saying 'Ooh, me bunions!' in a mock Benny Hill voice. That said, where I grew up we had a local Tory MP called Bill Benyon and for some reason – probably simple disdain for posh politicians, and possibly entirely unfairly – we sang a song at school about him that went 'Bill Benyon's got a bunion, and a face like a pickled onion'. That is all.

4.08 Warts & verrucas

Warts are papillomas (benign tumours of the skin or more rarely of mucous membranes) caused by infection by a human papillomavirus. There are lots of different types, from exotic long and thin filiform warts that are often found on the eyelids or lips, to more mundane rough, hard common warts (verruca vulgaris) that can crop up pretty much anywhere on the body. **They're very common and very hard to kill as the virus is resistant to drying and heat (it only dies at 100°C/212°F)**, although ultraviolet radiation helps.

Warts have been irritating humans for thousands of years: Hippocrates wrote about them in 400 BCE, but it wasn't until 1907 that the physician Giuseppe Ciuffo discovered that they were spread by a virus. Warts normally disappear without any treatment after a few months or years, although you can sometimes speed them on their way by freezing them off (cryotherapy) or using salicylic acid.

Warts rarely cause much more than annoyance or embarrassment, but there's one notorious foot version called a verruca (or verruca plantaris) that can be deep and painful. They sometimes have black specks in the middle of them and are often found on pressure points on the soles of your feet, making them particularly excruciating.

4.09 Wrinkles

No matter how much I tell you to love your wrinkles, you won't. Not really. So what are they? They're a £139 billion global market, expected to rise to a £306 billion global market by 2030, that's what they are, and the strongest driver of this market? The geriatric population.

Wrinkles are an inevitable part of the ageing process. There are various theories as to why they form, including misrepair-accumulation theory, but basically it all boils down to the fact that your skin is a complex organ that gets stretched and pulled all day and night as you move around, smile, snog and squash your face against the train window. On top of that, it's affected by an onslaught of hot–cold, weather-related contractions, drying from wind and heat, atmospheric and UV damage from the sun, erosional and depositional damage worthy of an alluvial flood plain, variations in the skin renovation process… let's face it, it's more surprising that your skin survives as well as it does.

So what is interesting about wrinkles? Well, **temporary water-immersion wrinkling, which occurs when you're in the bath for too long, is fun, and a surprisingly contested area of research**. Various studies have proved and then disproved that this weird wrinkling provides an evolutionary benefit by giving you better grip in the wet. Interestingly, if you cut certain nerves to the fingers, this wrinkling doesn't happen, meaning it's not just about osmosis (water entering the skin to balance electrolytes) but part of the nervous system. Right now this theory is in the 'proven' camp, but watch this space.

Chapter 05: Awkward Bits

5.01 Male nipples & vaginas

Men can lactate and even have tiny rudimentary vaginas. Oh, yes they do. But first let's discuss vestigial body parts – leftover scraps of body parts that serve no purpose. They're generally evolutionary echoes of a function that was once necessary for survival but is now obsolete. So why do we still have them? Mainly because getting rid of them isn't an evolutionary priority. If having nipples used metabolic energy or hindered men's reproduction in some way, they would almost certainly have been phased out, but if it ain't broke, why would evolution bother to fix it?

But why are nipples there in the first place? Well, it may surprise you to learn that we are all effectively born female. During the first few weeks of development, both male and female embryos follow similar genetic blueprints as they begin to create their body parts, including nipples and vaginas. It's only after six or seven weeks that a gene on the Y chromosome (which only males have) induces changes that kick-start testes development. At nine weeks, the foetus starts producing testosterone, which changes the genetic activity in the genitals and brain, stopping several organs, including the breasts, from developing. But now it's too late, mate – you've got nipples and nothin's gonna take 'em away.

It's not just nipples: all male mammals have rudimentary mammary glands and breast tissue, too – in fact all the apparatus needed for producing milk. After all, the word mammal comes from the Latin *mamma*, meaning breasts. The male Bismarck masked flying fox and dayak fruit bat can both lactate and there have been cases of human males lactating (not many, admittedly, but it's pretty well documented). It's thought that men lactate when the pituitary glands malfunction, overproducing hormones such as prolactin, which induces milk production.

In the appendix of testis, men even have tiny vestigial traces of a cervix, uterus and fallopian tubes. We also have a vestigial vagina: the vagina masculina (more prosaically known as the prostatic utricle), a duct in our genitals that goes nowhere. It's a remnant, admittedly, but what a remnant to have!

Other vestigial human body parts include the coccyx or 'tailbone' (see p102) as well as wisdom teeth and most of our body hair. The appendix also used to be considered utterly pointless but recent research indicates that it may be a source of beneficial gut bacteria. Vestigial body parts occur in other animals too, including wings on flightless birds, such as the cassowary, ostrich and kiwi. More weirdly, some whales have hind leg bones.

<u>Nippleology</u>

Both men and women can have polymastia, or supernumerary (more than two) nipples, and it's surprisingly widespread. Several celebrities sport them, including Harry Styles, Lily Allen and Tilda Swinton. There are quite a few studies on the phenomenon, although they show a rather suspect breadth of frequencies from 5.6% in German children to 0.22% in Hungarians, so methodology may not be particularly reliable. Supernumerary nipples are usually small and mole-like in appearance and found on the front of the torso, although they can appear anywhere, including on hands. They range from unusual areola-like colourations of the skin to full extra breasts – nipples with breast tissue underneath.

5.02 Menstrual blood

I t's odd that discussing menstruation is (in some cases) taboo, seeing as it's such a fundamental part of human existence – and truly amazing. For anyone who wasn't listening in biology lessons, every 28 days or so a woman's progesterone levels fall (unless they are pregnant), triggering the discharge of blood and mucosal tissue from the inner lining of the uterus via the vagina. This can last for two to seven days and is just another of the body's extraordinary cell-regeneration activities. **The amount of menstrual fluid discharged varies enormously but 35ml (1.2fl oz) per cycle is the average**. It's a dark red colour, and half of it is blood containing varying proportions of sodium, calcium, phosphate, iron and chloride. The rest is made up of dead endometrial tissue, protein-rich vaginal secretions and cervical mucus.

5.03 Faeces

Faeces sounds too formal, poo sounds too childish. But we'll go with faeces*. Lord knows why we're so afraid of discussing the latter stage of the digestive process – it's as essential as any of our other vital functions.

You normally produce 100–200g (3.5–7oz) of faeces every day, and depending on what you've eaten, your state of health, and the demographics of your microbiome population on any given day, it's usually 33.3% water and 66.6% solids. About 30% of your faeces is insoluble dietary fibre, including cellulose, and 30% is bacteria (both live and dead), but it also contains 10–20% inorganic matter such as calcium phosphate, 10–20% fatty lipids such as cholesterol, and 2–3% proteins, plus smaller amounts of dead cells from the lining of your guts, yellowy-brown stercobilin and urobilin produced from the remains of old red blood cells, and dead white blood cells. The Bristol Stool Scale is an excellent guide for communicating the state of your stool to interested parties without having to take a photograph and send it to them (which friends can find odd). It was developed at Bristol Royal Infirmary in 1997 and runs from the driest Type 1 'Separate hard lumps like nuts, hard to pass' through Type 4 'Like a sausage or snake, smooth and soft' to Type 7 'Watery, no solid pieces; entirely liquid'. Mine are currently firmly in the healthy-but-dull Type 4 camp, although I prefer to range up and down the scale whenever possible as befits a diverse diet**.

*By the way, I urge you to put this down immediately and rush out to buy a copy of *Fartology* (Quadrille), also by me, which goes into great detail about faeces and even greater detail about farts.

**Most doctors, however, are very clear that they'd like you to stick to Types 3–5.

You have not one but two sphincters at the end of your rectum via which you deposit your poo: an internal one that you have no voluntary control over and an external one that you do. Incidentally, **when you have to strain to push a reluctant poo out of the door, you're carrying out the splendidly named Valsalva manoeuvre**. It's an attempt to breathe out whilst keeping your glottis closed, which builds up pressure in the chest cavity and abdomen to help push down on the contents of your rectum, but it also raises your blood pressure and kicks off some wildly complex cardiovascular activity. Be careful when you deploy it. All that pressure can result in hiatal hernia or even cardiac arrest, and the brief drop in blood pressure after you release the squeeze can itself cause a blackout.

Poo can be very useful. It's a great fertilizer and I've seen walls in rural India plastered in cow pats being dried to be used as fuel for fires. On the downside, every single gram of your poo is packed with 40 billion bacteria and 100 million archaea (single-celled organisms without a nucleus), some of which can be dangerous. Poo is usually the main cause of cholera outbreaks, so care needs to be taken if you use it to grow food.

<u>Poo-ology</u>

Some people, including me, can turn their poo bright red by eating beetroot. This is because we don't fully break down the purple betanin pigment that gives beetroot its colour. If you forgot that you ate beetroot the night before or it was hidden in your hummus, it can be terrifying! Mine goes a deep, dramatic A&E-style blood red, although my pee doesn't change colour, which is a shame.

5.04 Urine

Depending on diet and levels of physical activity, women produce about 1 litre (1.8 pints) of urine every day whereas men produce about 1.4 litres (2.5 pints). It's a fantastic tool for getting rid of water-soluble waste, especially nitrogen-rich substances that your cells have generated as by-products of cellular respiration. These include urea (widely used as a fertilizer), uric acid (which can cause gout if you have too much in your blood) and creatinine (a by-product of muscle metabolism). **All this nitrogen means that your pee is a fabulous fertilizer, and your garden would thank you for a good dousing with it**. You can also mix it together with manure to create potassium nitrate – an essential ingredient in gunpowder, alongside sulphur and charcoal.

The formal word for taking a pee is micturition. The urine you produce is slightly acidic (around pH 6.2) and usually about 95% water. It's yellow due to the compound urobilin, which is made by the breakdown of old red blood cells. Some people's urine can turn pink after eating beetroot because their bodies don't break down the bright red betanin compound that gives beets their rich colour. Asparagus contains sulphurous compounds that can break down to give your pee a rich, funky, earthy smell.

There have been lots of fascinating uses for urine throughout history. It has been used as a cleaning fluid, teeth whitener and for cleaning clothes in ancient Rome – mainly because the urea breaks down into ammonia, which is great for cleaning and also strongly antiseptic. There's a traditional Chinese dish called *tong zi dan*, or 'virgin boy egg', which is an egg soaked, boiled and then cured in urine collected from young boys. It's supposed to be good for your health.

Peeology

So, what is urine NOT good for? Well, contrary to popular belief, it doesn't help with jellyfish stings for starters. And despite the many health claims made for auto-urine therapy (drinking your own urine) there's no scientific evidence to back it up. It's not a great idea to drink too much urine because, in spite of what you might have heard, it's not sterile, it contains various toxins, and it's packed with all those nitrogen-rich compounds that your body has put lots of effort into getting rid of. And what about drinking it in desperation when you're suffering from dehydration? Sadly, due to the high level of dissolved salts in urine, this is likely to be counterproductive.

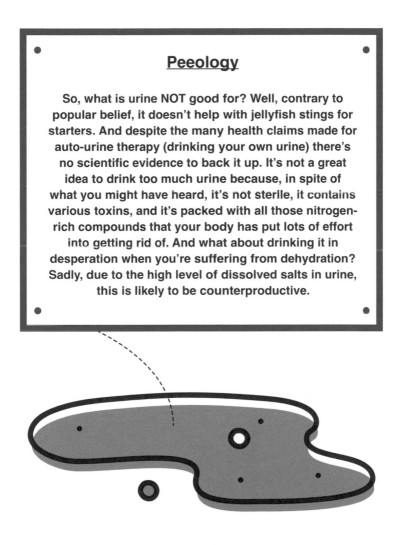

5.05 Invisible human rubbish

Y ou produce a lot of waste, but much of it is invisible. During cellular respiration a sequence of metabolic reactions takes place in every cell in your body that uses oxygen to break down glucose fuel extracted from food to obtain chemical energy. It's a combustion reaction and, as with an engine in a petrol-driven car, it creates carbon dioxide (CO_2) and water as waste products. You can't see or smell CO_2 but you create quite a lot of it: the atmospheric air you breath in contains 0.04% CO_2 but the air you breathe out contains 4%*. It's effectively your exhaust gas.

Your body is in a continual state of renewal. Your skin constitutes 16% of your body weight and its outer layer is completely replaced every month. Red blood cells are renewed every four months, taste-bud cells every 10 days, and the small intestine lining every two to four days. Ten per cent of the cells in your skeleton are replaced every year. Fat cells, rather annoyingly, last a full eight years, but only a handful of tissues stay the same for your whole life, including the lens of your eye. Bits of you are constantly falling off or being excreted in your various juices. Many cells are also eaten by your own phagocytes, which then expel waste matter such as membrane proteins, soluble proteins, hormones and lipids into plasma using a process called exocytosis, and this is then either recycled or squirted out of you one way or another.

*Despite the claims of climate sceptics, your breath doesn't add to greenhouse gas emissions – it's just part of the cycle of photosynthesis that converted water and CO_2 into oxygen and storable energy to bring you your food. When you breathe out you're simply returning that same CO_2 and water back into the atmosphere.

Researchers at the Weizmann Institute of Science in Rehovot, Israel, calculated that about **330 billion of your cells are replaced every day** – that's over 1% of all your cells. Your gorgeous body contains around 30 trillion human cells, so you create the equivalent of a new you every 90 days or so.

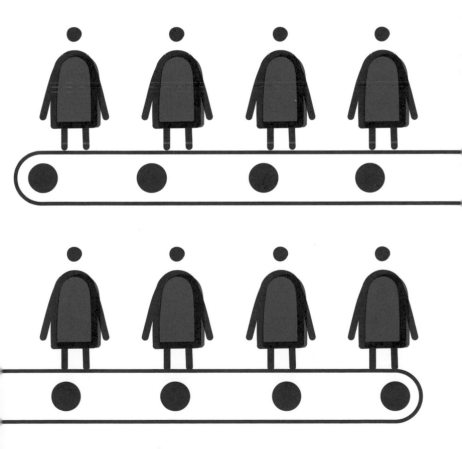

5.06 Belly button

Like any normal person, I fiddle with my belly button constantly throughout the day*. Also known as the umbilicus, it's simply scar tissue made up of the remnants of your umbilical cord that attached you to your mother's placenta. Although all placental mammals are supposed to have one**, I've never found my dog's.

The umbilical cord supplies an unborn baby with nutrients and oxygen, and transports waste away. **It's made up of two arteries and a vein covered in a delightfully named gooey substance called Wharton's jelly**, which collapses the umbilical cord after birth, effectively closing it off within about three minutes.

Soon after birth the umbilical cord is clamped and then cut with scissors, which appears horribly dramatic at the time but as it contains no nerves, the baby doesn't feel it. (The inside remnant of the cord that makes up your belly button also doesn't have any feeling. Go on, give yours a poke. I just did. Nothing.) The small stump of cord left behind changes to a range of delightful colours before turning black and falling off, usually around two weeks after birth. Though the temptation to make it into a key ring is strong, it really is best to pop it in the compost bin.

*Tell me it's not just me. Some people suffer from omphalophobia, which has nothing to do with Willy Wonka's industrious staff, but everything to do with a fear of belly buttons.

**So many mammals are placental that it's easier to list the ones that aren't – they are from the order Monotremata, a gorgeous group that includes the platypuses and echidna, and the infraclass Marsupialia, which have fabulous names such as wombats, numbats, possums, pig-footed bandicoots and kangaroos.

Buttonology

In 2012, researchers at North Carolina State University undertook the Belly Button Diversity Project to investigate the microbes living inside our navels. They took samples from hundreds of people and found 2,300 different types of bacteria in the first 60 samples alone, many of them unique to the single person on which they were found. The results uncovered lots of very common *Staphylococcus epidermidis* bacteria as well as bright yellow *Micrococcus luteus* and *Pseudomonas*. They also discovered that only 4% of the participants had outies.

Navel oranges have a 'belly button' opposite their stem due to an underdeveloped second fruit growing nested in the peel of the primary fruit.

5.07 Bruises & love bites

Bruises

Known as contusions in medical terminology, bruises are tissue haematomas (areas of internal bleeding) where some form of trauma has caused red blood cells to leak out of the capillaries carrying them and into surrounding tissue.

One of the most intriguing things about bruises is their changing colour, which is all down to a sequence of catabolic 'breakdown' reactions that dismantle the leaked blood. The haemoglobin in red blood cells initially makes your skin look red, black and blue – the skin tends to absorb more red light and reflect more blue light to our eyes (which is why the veins on your hands also look blue). Once the red blood cells are outside the capillaries, they no longer work properly and need to be purged by your body, so phagocytes arrive to consume them. As these phagocytes break down the haemoglobin in the red blood cells, a series of reactions begins, first creating biliverdin, which makes the bruise look green. Next phagocytes break the biliverdin down into bilirubin (one of the pigments that makes our pee yellow), turning the bruise yellow, before breaking that down into iron-storing hemosiderin, which gives the bruise a brown colour.

Love bites

Love bites are simply bruises created by suction instead of impact, and depending on your point of view, they are either a symbol of rebellion, a bad boy/girl badge to annoy your parents with, or an idiotic sign of immaturity and desperation. If you really want to make an evolutionary case for them, you could point out that many animals, including cats, bite each others' necks before and during mating.

Many magazines offer advice for magically getting rid of love bites but it's all useless apart from the mundane RICE (Rest, Ice, Compression, Elevation) bruise treatment. **As long as you're healthy, they will disappear in around two weeks, like any other bruise**. There are reports of a New Zealand woman who was given a small hickey next to a major artery that led to a blood clot that then travelled to her heart and caused a stroke, but she is reported to have made a full recovery. So that's all right, then.

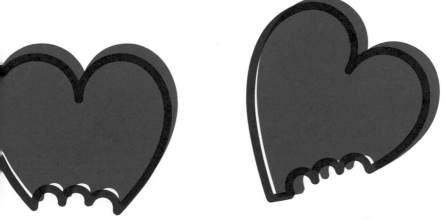

5.08 Snogging

The scientific term for kissing is osculation and, depending on your own particular technique, it uses around 34 facial muscles, including the circular orbicularis oris complex in the lips surrounding the mouth (**your lips are actually a sphincter. This is possibly my favourite fact of all time**). Many species kiss, including chimps and bonobos, whilst my dog gives me licks when I come home (though this might simply be because I laugh and show him lots of affection when he does). But, of course, we're not talking about a peck on the cheek here, we're talking about romantic kissing: snogging, with tongues and everything.

The science of kissing is called philematology and although it's been extensively studied, **we don't know the fundamental reason why humans kiss, especially when it's so dangerous**. You can exchange all manner of bacteria and catch diseases such as colds, syphilis and herpes simplex from kissing and exchanging saliva, so you'd think it shouldn't offer an evolutionary advantage. It's also unclear whether we kiss instinctively or if it's a learned behaviour that we copy from our parents and peers.

What we do know is that it involves a combination of biology and psychology, and is important in selecting a partner. A study in *Evolutionary Psychology* showed that kissing a prospective partner can be a deal-breaker, and that women kiss 'to establish and monitor the status of their relationship, and to assess and periodically update the level of commitment on the part of a partner'. Men, on the other hand, 'tended to kiss as a means to an end – to gain sexual favors or to reconcile'. The authors concluded that this meant kissing was a 'mate-assessment technique' – to which every teenager reading this is thinking: 'No shit, Sherlock'.

Kissing kick-starts a lot of mood-enhancing biochemistry, stimulating the release of oxytocin (associated with feelings of love, social bonding and sexual attraction), dopamine (associated with pleasure) and endorphins (associated with happiness), and suppressing stress-related cortisol. Studies have found that more frequent kissing, even when researchers simply told the subjects to kiss more frequently (rather than because the subjects felt like it), improved 'perceived stress, relationship satisfaction, and total serum cholesterol.'

Snogology

A proper snog is likely to transfer a billion bacteria from one person to another, alongside about 0.5mg salt, 0.5mg protein, 0.7mcg of fat and 0.2mcg of assorted food and... stuff.

5.09 Nutcracker

There's nothing like a wallop in the crotch to bring a man to his knees. For ladies reading this, a nutcracker causes men to experience a strange rising sense of pain and panic with a weird twist: the pain is felt more in the abdomen than in the testicles (the panic comes from the suspicion that their chances of becoming a father might finally be over). A nutcrack can be so painful that the sufferer vomits, although for some reason their friends find it enormously amusing.

The reason for all the drama and confused pain centres is that the abdomen and scrotum share a set of nerves and tissues. **The testicles develop inside the abdominal cavity while the baby is in the womb and then descend into the scrotum at about three to six months**, but a strong physical connection remains. Things get worse if the impact causes a twisting of the spermatic cord – called testicular torsion – which can cut off the blood supply, making it really bloody serious indeed and can you please stop laughing?

And why is it so painful? Well, the testicles are a crucial part of the reproductive process but also precariously external, so in a desperate attempt to protect them evolution has supplied men with a high concentration of nerve endings there. This makes them extremely sensitive and even a gentle tap on the testicles is a painful alarm bell that tells their owner to take more care of them. All things considered, it's quite surprising that they developed outside the body at all, although there are several theories. Sperm production requires a narrow temperature range that's cooler than our usual 37°C

(98.6°F) internal body temperature, but no one seems to know why a different adaptation didn't develop – most mammals have internal testes, as do birds (whose core body temperature is very high), so there are likely to be other reasons. Maybe the ladies simply liked the look of them? I mean 'used them as a sexual selection tool'.

<u>Nutcrackology</u>

If you've been nutcracked, the pain should subside within an hour, but if it lasts longer or you see bruising, it's off to the doc's with you. There are specialist groups of people who enjoy and actively seek out the sensation of a well-deployed nutcracker, but that really is a story for another book.

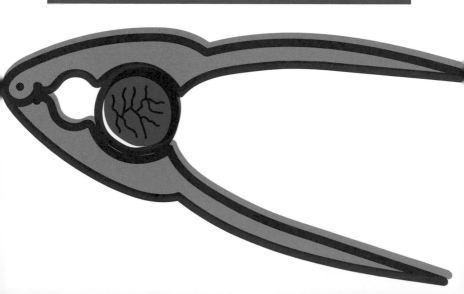

5.10 Human tails

You're probably aware that the coccyx at the base of the spine is the faint evolutionary echo of our ape ancestors' tails, but did you know you once owned a surprisingly large prenatal tail? **Yes, after four to five weeks in the womb your embryo had between 10 and 12 enthusiastically developing vertebrae in a spectacular tail measuring one-sixth of your entire size.** But then the most bizarre thing happened: it began to disappear. It's as though your genes suddenly remembered that they were creating a human and not a Labrador and simply decided to ditch the tail despite the effort already put into it.

It turns out that your genetic blueprint contains more elements than are required to create the final version of you, so they're simply switched off and pre-programmed cell death (called apoptosis) kicks in. By the eighth week of gestation the sixth to eighth vertebrae and their surrounding tissues are killed off and eventually all that's left is your coccyx.

Very rarely, however, this tail regression isn't completed because the gene that should have been switched off gets reactivated and the tail starts growing again. This results in a baby born with a small version of a tail, complete with muscle, connective tissue, normal skin and hair follicles. A *BMJ* Case Report from 2012 has details of a three-month-old baby girl born with a spectacular 11cm (4in) tail that was successfully removed. What's most unsettling about the tail was that it looked like a very long, thin finger and didn't stick out directly from the coccyx but a little over to the left of it. It also grew alarmingly fast, reaching 11cm (4in) by the age of three months. Thankfully the condition is very rare, with only 40 cases ever recorded.

5.11 Arse

can't imagine another body part, other than our genitals, that
we find so embarrassing to reveal to others as our beautifully
engineered, puckered, hairy arses. Why on earth should the mouth
be so revered in great poetry while the anus is so trenchantly
ignored? I guess it's because delicious, finely wrought things tend to
go into the mouth and foul-stinking primal faeces emerge from the
arse, but you can't really have one without the other.

'Arse' is not, obviously, a technical term but rather a general word
for a collection of body parts with several distinct sections, including
the rectum, anus, sphincter and buttocks. The rectum is simply the
internal holding chamber for your faeces (see p87), collecting them
up and sending messages to your brain about how full it is, and how
you should start preparing reading matter, smelly candles and a calm
space in which to offload. The anus itself opens out to your inner
and outer sphincters, the final stage of the digestive system, used
for getting rid of solid waste. **Birds, reptiles and amphibians
do not have a separate anus, urinary tract and vagina, and
instead have a much simpler device called a cloaca**, which
they used for both solid and liquid waste, for sex and for laying eggs.

Chapter 06:
Hairy Humans

6.01 You are hairy

All mammals are hairy to some extent (even the absurdly ugly naked mole rat* has a few pubey hairs), though humans are some of the least hairy. Hair's main function was to keep our ancestors warm and you have around 5 million strands of it across your entire body, most of which grow around 0.4mm (0.02in) every day. This may sound like a lot of hair but the number pales into insignificance compared with a beaver's 10 billion hairs and a hairstreak butterfly's 100 billion.

Humans are unique among primates for having lost so much hair during their evolution and it's not clear why this happened. Genetic evidence indicates that we stopped being furry around 1.7 million years ago. It's possible that human hairiness was reduced to a post-puberty, secondary sex characteristic that announced when we were ready to reproduce. **One intriguing notion is that humans lost their hair as a result of ectoparasites such as fleas**. As we became a more social species and lived more closely together, fleas and lice would have become more of a problem – shedding the hair they cosied up in would have helped avoid damaging infestations. Another theory suggests that hair may have become a liability as we discovered the use of fire – unhairy humans would have been less likely to immolate themselves – but it's a bit tenuous.

As you'll discover while reading this section, what we don't know about hair far outweighs what we do. The reasons why some hair is curly and some straight, why we get dandruff, and why pubes are so wiry are all mysteries to science.

*The only mammalian thermoconformer – like insects, the naked mole rat doesn't bother to regulate its body temperature and is effectively cold-blooded.

That said, all hair follows the same basic biology. It sprouts from follicles sunk deep in the skin where cells divide and multiply, pushing out hair from your dermal papillae a little like toothpaste from a tube. Your hair grows faster in summer than in winter and in technical terms it's known as stratified squamous keratinized epithelium. Stratified means that it's arranged in layers of filaments, squamous means that the surface cells are flattened, and keratinized epithelium is a type of animal tissue made of keratin, an extraordinary fibrous protein that's the basis of many tough-yet-flexible animal parts, including hair, nails, claws and hooves.

Hair is effectively dead because there's no biochemical activity going on in it, but let's take a cross-section of a hair strand and look inside. It consists of three main concentric rings: the soft, delicate, relatively unstructured medulla in the centre is surrounded by the cortex that provides the strength and structure of the strand as well as its colour (which depends on its melanin content). Then comes the cuticle outer casing, which is covered in a layer of oily, waterproof lipid just a single molecule thick.

Hair growth is a gloriously quirky cycle. Every strand on your body is at one of three stages of development: a long anagen growth phase during which hair grows, a short catagen breakdown phase as the follicle shrinks, and a telogen resting phase as the hair is shed and a new one begins to grow.

6.02 Head hair

Your head packs 100,000–150,000 strands of thick, long terminal hair onto your scalp (terminal hair is also found on pubic areas, underarms and beards). Each one is 0.017–0.018mm (0.00067–0.00071in) wide, and can grow as long as 1m (3ft). Like all hair follicles, your head-hair follicles are always at one of three stages: growth, breakdown or dormancy, but head hair has a longer growth period than most, at six years or so, during which it grows at a rate of around 0.4mm (0.02in) a day or 1cm (0.4in) a month*. This is followed by a two-week breakdown phase and a dormant period of six months or so before growth begins again. The maximum length of head hair is usually limited to around 1m (3ft) because it eventually falls out as a result of the cyclical growth pattern. But you'll grow a total of 8m (26ft) of head hair over your lifetime.

Head hair is also an indicator of relative health, youth and subculture** and can help with sexual selection. Humans have been obsessed with how their hair looks for thousands of years. In 2003 Clonycavan Man was discovered in a peat bog in Ireland. The hair on this well-preserved Iron Age body's head was raised up with the help of a hair tie and hair gel made from plant oil and pine resin imported from northern Spain or south-west France.

*There's a wide range – from 0.6cm (0.2in) to 3.4cm (1.3in) a month – with thicker hair growing faster than thinner hair.
**My personal subculture is currently 'scruffy nerd', although I have tried punk, Bright Young Thing and an awful *fin de siècle* girl-boy Led Zep look in my tweens. None has ever really cut the mustard.

Dandruff

Around half of all adults get dandruff, but no one really knows why and there's no known cure, though you can spend an awful lot of money on products that claim to help. Particularly bad cases can be a result of the skin disorder seborrheic dermatitis (if you have redness and itching around the nose and eyebrows as well as the scalp, you probably have this) but no one knows the cause of that either, although a yeast called *Malassezia* is thought to be involved. We do know that the basic problem is overproduction and over-shedding of skin cells, and that dandruff scales are made of keratin protein. The best treatments seem to be coal tar and antifungal shampoos.

Baldness

Baldness affects a quarter of men by the age of 30, half of men by the age of 45 and a quarter of all women by the age of 50. Humans are one of only two primates that routinely suffer from it – the other is an old world monkey species called the stump-tailed macaque. Bald people have the same number of follicles as hairy people but theirs have stopped functioning properly and produce only colourless, thin hairs. Male-pattern baldness starts with a receding front hairline and hair loss on the crown of the head, followed by a general retreat of the cavalry. It's caused by changing androgen hormones that define male characteristics, as well as genetic predisposition. Female-pattern baldness is typically a generalized thinning across the scalp and its causes are a mystery. Alopecia areata is a slightly different type of hair loss, usually localized and unpredictable.

6.03 Body hair

Although you're the least hairy of all mammals with a mere 5 million strands, you still grow a wide variety of hairs, including one you only briefly had – and ate – while in the womb. This first hair is lanugo, a downy, thick and colourless layer that starts to grow on the foetus at 12–16 weeks. It's usually shed into the amniotic fluid in the womb a month or so before birth, although it can occasionally stick around for a few weeks afterwards.

In the womb the foetus drinks amniotic fluid and so actively consumes the shed hair, which then forms part of the first startling meconium poo that babies deliver straight after they're born to give their parents a clear sign that this parenting thing ain't gonna be anywhere near as tidy as it looks in the nappy ads.

A few months after birth, vellus hair (or 'down' hair) begins to grow over most of the body. It's fine and short (less than 2mm (0.08in), and appears everywhere except for your palms, the soles of your feet and places such as the lips. Strangely its follicles aren't connected to a sebaceous gland.

During and after puberty you start to grow tougher androgenic terminal hair prompted by hormones called androgens, and it's thicker and more widespread on men than women. This is when other weird and wonderful hairs also start to grow on your body: facial hair, pubic hair, and various different grades across legs, armpits, eyebrows, chest, buttocks, genitals and shoulders. Leg hairs are relatively short because most only grow for about two months (as opposed to six years or so for head hair). Armpit hairs have a longer growth phase of around six months.

<u>Hairology</u>

A study published in 2018 looked at how our follicles produce either curly or straight hair but failed to come to a conclusion, so I won't waste your time dragging you through it. The researchers identified that circular hair shafts produce straighter hair and oval shafts produce curlier hair, but couldn't work out why.

Contrary to popular opinion, cutting, waxing or shaving your hair has no effect whatsoever on what happens at the root.

Hypertrichosis causes excessive body hair to grow in strange places, while hirsutism causes women to have thicker terminal hair in places where it usually grows on men, such as the chest or face.

6.04 Nose & ear hair

Nose hair

I have long, thick, luxuriant nasal hair that, tragically, I need to trim to reduce excessive sneezing events. Your nasal hair follicles have relatively short cycles compared to head hair, but over the course of your life each can grow a total of 2m (6.5ft) of hair.

Nose hair is thought to filter out unwanted matter (dust, pollen, flies, whipped cream and the like) to stop it heading down to the delicate machinery of your lungs. But this theory is undermined by the fact that women on average seem to have less nose hair yet still thrive despite having lungs – presumably – packed with dust, pollen and flies. That said, there is strong evidence that people who suffer from hay fever and other seasonal allergies who have heavier nose hair density are less likely to develop asthma than those with lighter nose hair density, so it does seem that these hairs serve a purpose.

Ear hair

Ear hair is a completely different beast, made up of two different hair types: soft downy vellus (see p109) that covers most of the ear, and additional thick terminal tragi hairs on the outer tragus, antitragus and helix sections of the ear, seen most clearly on men. We have no idea what this hair is for other than scaring small children and keeping the ear warm, but helix hair growth is found to be particularly prevalent on some Indian men. The Guinness World Record for the longest ear hair is held by Radhakant Bajpai, an Indian grocer, whose ear hair measured 13.2cm (5in) when he won the record in 2003. By the time of a 2009 interview it had reached 25cm (10in).

If you want to tame your ear or nasal hair, beware. There's little that compares with the agony of pulling out a nose hair and there's a danger of developing an ingrown hair, which is very bad indeed. Each time you pull out a hair (or aggressively pick your nose) you risk creating a small cut near the nasal cavity that could become infected. Sinus infections can be exceedingly painful, so standard advice is to trim, not pluck, and in any case, it's best to leave a nice crud-catching thatch.

6.05 Armpit hair

Despite the fact that armpit hair starts growing at puberty, it's not a type of pubic hair, but axillary hair. Little is known about its evolutionary function but it's thought to reduce chafing by providing a rolling layer between arm and chest (though people who shave it off don't seem to develop any problems). It never grows particularly long because it has a growth cycle of only six months.

Axillary hair serves to anchor the various smells generated by bacteria that feed on the fatty sweat produced by apocrine sweat glands in our armpits. This gives us all a unique smell, which may be attractive to the opposite sex, and may also produce pheromones (although evidence for the existence and perception of pheromones in humans is pretty much non-existent, see p117). Like you, I adore the smell of my own armpits after a heavy, stressful day but others in my household are less enthusiastic, despite me citing a 2018 study that found that women who smelled a partner's shirt and then took part in tests found those tests less stressful. There's no pleasing some people.

A 2016 study found that men who shaved their armpits significantly reduced their body odour for the next 24 hours. Other studies have found that women tend to find the smell of men with high testosterone more attractive when they're in the most fertile phase of their menstrual cycle, and that men think that women smell best when they're most fertile.

6.06 Facial hair

Men's facial hair is a physiologically pointless, testosterone-driven quirk peculiar to humans (gorilla and chimpanzee facial hair gets thinner rather than thicker as they age). Beard shape and thickness are mainly driven by the EDAR gene and beard growth is a secondary sex characteristic, meaning that it isn't a fundamental part of the reproductive system but, like deer antlers, lion manes and peacock tails, is a product of sexual selection, functioning as an ornamental sign to females that a male has strong genes to pass on to their offspring.

Which brings us to the big question: do women prefer a man with a beard? According to a 2014 study published in *Biology Letters*, women have 'negative frequency-dependent preferences', meaning that if the majority of men on offer are clean-shaven they prefer men with beards, but if the majority have beards, they prefer men who are clean-shaven*. Typical.

*A twist to this story is a 2013 study in which researchers discovered that heavy stubble was the most attractive look, and that women at the most fertile stage of their menstrual cycle found it most attractive.

6.07 Eyebrows & eyelashes

Eyebrows

It's not entirely clear why humans have eyebrows. On our ancestors they may have stopped sweat and rain from dripping into the eyes, and possibly shielded them from the sun. Take a look at our ancestor *Homo heidelbergensis*, with her magnificent brow ridge but practically non-existent forehead, and this theory doesn't seem as ridiculous as it first sounds. She practically had a baseball cap made of bone.

But humans' tiny brow ridges are completely useless as hairy baseball caps, so why do we still have them? Well, **eyebrows are a surprisingly powerful communication tool, capable of conveying a remarkably nuanced range of meanings**. Alongside your relatively enormous forehead with its elastic skin controlled by a range of muscles, they are very useful for intensifying expressions and conveying complex empathy.

Picture the *Mona Lisa*. It's hard not to be beguiled by that face and confused by that expression. Is it love? Disdain? Has she decided her day would have been better if only she'd done a good poo? We can't tell because she has no eyebrows. Leonardo da Vinci's genius – alongside a tasty bit of brushwork – was to remove those telltale emotional signposts to leave us guessing. If the eyes are a window to the soul, the eyebrows are a window into the emotions.

Eyelashes

Eyelashes seem to have a much clearer protective function. Your upper lid contains 90–160 individual curved lashes laid out in five or six rows, while the lower lid has 75–80 lashes in three to four rows. The mechanoreceptors at their root make them intensely touch-sensitive, forcing you to blink reflexively if they're activated by a foreign object such as a fly or speck of dust. They also have a remarkable effect on the aerodynamics around the eye, slowing the evaporation of your tear film and reducing the amount of particles falling onto the eyeball. A wind tunnel study showed that the optimum length of an eyelash is one-third the width of the eye*.

*Can someone please tell my eyelash-loving daughter Poppy this because, like any teenager worth their salt, she won't listen to me.

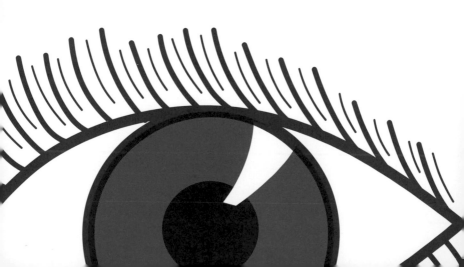

6.08 Pubic hair

We're not sure why humans are so hairless (see p109), but to make matters more complicated, we have this mysterious bush of pubes sprouting around our genitals. **Most primates have finer hair around their genitals than on the rest of their body, so why we have this thatch of strange wiry hairs around ours is one of the many unanswered questions of human evolution**.

Pubes are formed of thick terminal body hair and grow after puberty* as a result of increased hormone production. Back when communication was more grunt-based, they may have played a signalling role, providing a visual indication that another human had reached puberty and thus mating with them would have an evolutionary benefit.

Some have suggested that pubic hair reduces chafing on the genitals and friction during sex (though some also say that the friction is the best bit), while others say a decent bush may trap and nurture pheromones that could be attractive to the opposite sex. There are a few holes in this latter theory: 1) no human pheromone molecules have ever been found, 2) even if they do exist we don't know if humans can smell them, and 3) we don't have a vomeronasal organ – the secondary nose that dogs, cats and many other mammals seem to use to detect pheromones.

*Puberty is not, despite what two girls named Daisy and Poppy have asserted, the age at which you are allowed to accompany your parents to the pub. Rather, it is a widespread set of physical changes by which the human body matures to become an adult capable of reproduction.

Pubic hair does trap dirt and sweat, which may be useful to stop these getting into the penis or vagina – body openings that are susceptible to incoming pathogens. Pubic hair also insulates the genitals, which is handy, but if other primates can do without it, why not us?

Pubeology

Pondering the point of pubes is pointless, so instead let us consider merkins. Merkins are pubic wigs, thought to have been originally used by prostitutes to cover the scars of sexually transmitted diseases, or to hide the fact that they had shaved their pubic hair to control lice. Now, though, they are more commonly used by actors as small but psychologically significant 'furry bikinis' when performing nude scenes, or to show a more natural look common to earlier eras – or simply to cover up the fact that they got carried away with the mower.

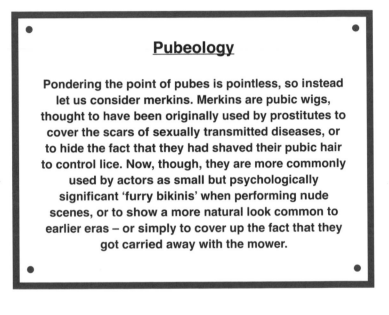

6.09 Nails & cuticles

I n 2014 Guinness World Records measured the fingernails on Shridhar Chillal's left hand and concluded that they had a cumulative length of 909.6cm (358in), including a 197.8cm (78in) thumbnail curled into a tight ball. It's surely the most impractical world record to break.

Fingernails start developing in the womb at about 20 weeks and they're made of tough, flexible keratin protein cells formed at the active tissue matrix in the nail root. As new cells are produced, they're pushed forward by cells developing behind them, forming the nail plate that slides out along the nail bed. This bed contains lots of blood vessels, which supply the plate itself with nutrients. It also contains lots of nerves, which is why it's so painful if you rip or cut the living section of the nail. Fingernails grow at an average rate of 3.5mm (0.1in) a month but toenails grow more slowly at about 1.6mm (0.06in) a month. Nails stop growing when you die, although dehydrating skin on a dead body can make the adjacent skin retract, making it look like your nails have kept growing.

<u>Autocannibalology</u>

I'm always biting and eating my cuticles, sometimes to the extent that they are painful and bleeding. It's an autocannibalism disorder known as dermatophagia, and there seems to be no pattern to it: I do it when I'm bored or stressed, as well as when I'm not bored or stressed. I just really, really like it, and get an immense sense of satisfaction when I tear off a particularly large section of skin, followed swiftly by the realization that I'm an idiot as it's now going to hurt for weeks. Oddly, I don't bite my nails, and I think that people who do are weird.

We are all autocannibals to some extent, producing and eating a huge variety of different substances, including saliva, nasal mucus and dead cells from our tongues and cheeks. Some of us like sucking blood from cuts and chewing scabs, too. But the most enthusiastic autocannibal is probably the North American rat snake, one of which was found in the wild having consumed about two-thirds of its own body. When my dog and cat chase their tails, I always wonder how far things could go.

6.10 Tongue hair

Black hairy tongue is surprisingly common, affecting around 13% of the population. It's a strangely dark, hairlike coating on the surface of the tongue towards the back of mouth and it's due to overgrown filiform papillae. These nipple-like, touch-sensitive, cone-shaped structures are covered in brush-like threads and found all over the tongue but don't contain any taste sensors. They normally cover the tongue to a height of 1mm (0.04in) but can become overgrown, especially at the back of the tongue, if they aren't rubbed down by brushing or normal abrasive action. If they get particularly long, they can look like hairs (after all, they are made of the same stuff: keratin), and can trap bacteria, food and yeasts. When this happens, the microbes change the skin colour to black, white, brown or even green. Poor toothbrush-work and extensive use of antibiotics or other medications are two possible causes of black hairy tongue. Symptoms are rare, though it can lead to halitosis (see p140). It's usually quite easy to get rid of the hairs using a toothbrush and a tongue scraper.

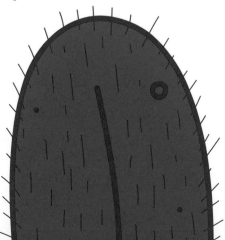

Chapter 07: Your Cozy Parasite Family

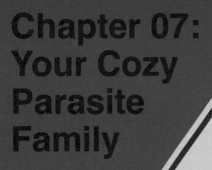

7.01 Bacteria

You are never alone. Far from it. You are teeming with bacteria, inside and out. So many bacteria, in fact, that you may be more bacteria than human: **a 70kg (154lb) person contains around 30 trillion human cells (the vast majority of which, around 85%, are red blood cells) and around 39 trillion bacteria, viruses and fungi***. These make up the personal world of microbes known as your microbiome, which is both vital to human health and a source of disease. And smells. The bacteria it contains are tiny compared to human cells and only live for an average of 20 minutes. Collectively they weigh just 200g (7oz) but they multiply ferociously fast and crop up all over your body, with a major concentration in your gut. You also have 100,000 microbes per cm^2 (0.16 sq in) of skin, from 200 different species.

Bacteria were first spotted in 1676 by the Dutch cloth merchant Anthonie van Leeuwenhoek while looking at raindrops under his microscope. He noticed little wriggly things in the raindrops and named them 'animalcules', which was sweet. It wasn't until 1844 that Agostino Bassi discovered that they weren't all sweet, but sometimes caused disease. Then in 1876 Robert Koch discovered that they could cause disease in humans – namely anthrax.

Bacteria are single-celled organisms that are usually rod-shaped or spherical, and most are harmless or even beneficial to us, especially the ones in your gut that help you digest food (these provide about

*It used to be thought we contained an even greater proportion of bacteria to human cells, in a ratio of 10:1, but that was re-assessed in a 2016 study by Ron Milo and Ron Sender at the Weizmann Institute of Science in Rehovot, Israel, and Shai Fuchs at the Hospital for Sick Children in Toronto, Canada.

10% of your calories by breaking down foods your gut wouldn't be able to tackle on its own). Over 1 million microbial species have been identified but less than 1,500 are known to cause human diseases. However, the ones that do, such as the bacteria behind cholera, typhoid, plague and tuberculosis, can be devastating when they multiply in large numbers. About one-third of all human deaths are caused by microbes.

You are particularly good at spreading bacteria yourself. You touch your face an average 16 times every hour, helping to transmit microbes from the environment to your bodily orifices, and microbes from your face back to the environment. That said, they're picky buggers and certain parts of the body tend to be home to very specific types of bacteria.

Your bacterial body
Estimates vary, but you're probably carrying around 40,000 different species of microbes across your body. Here are a few of them:

Scalp
Dandruff is mostly caused by the changing balance of *Propionibacterium* and *Staphylococcus*.

Mouth
Streptococcus mutans turns sugars into acid that attacks tooth enamel and causes cavities. It's just one of 1,300 different species of bacteria on your gums and 800 on the inside of your cheeks.

Nose

The nostrils contain around 900 different species.

Skin

Propionibacterium acnes inhabit skin pores and hair follicles and can cause spots. At least 200 different species live here.

Armpit

Staphylococcus hominis produces stinking compounds called thioalcohols, when it encounters sweat.

Vagina

Mainly *Lactobacillus* bacteria, which produces lactic acid, but also *Candida albicans*, the fungus behind thrush.

Gut

The majority of our microbiome lives here: around 36,000 different species.

Poo

About 30% of solid waste is dead bacteria.

Feet

Staphylococcus epidermidis always seems to be present with isovaleric acid – the smell of elderly Stilton cheese.

7.02 You are mouldy

Moulds and yeasts are all fungi, and they are everywhere in our environment, although in humans they mainly affect the skin, gut, respiratory tract and genitourinary tract. Familiar yeast infections include vaginal thrush and ringworm but *Candida* species are also found harmlessly in your gut. Fungi cell walls are very tough, which makes them difficult to tackle. About 300 types can cause relatively minor infections in humans (although these can be more serious for immune-deficient patients) – **in general fungi are a lot more problematic for the plant world**. Exceptions include *Cryptococcus neoformans*, which causes severe meningitis, and *Stachybotrys chartarum* (the 'landlord' mould that crept up the damp walls of my student accommodation), which causes headaches and respiratory damage.

7.03 Parasites (Trigger Warning)

The number one nightmare of all children across the world is finding a parasitic worm breaking through their skin and wriggling out covered in blood and pus. Do you just let it ooze out on its own and risk it disappearing back inside? Or do you grab its head and tug, running the danger of tearing it in two and leaving half of it inside you forever?

Various endoparasites can be found inside the human body, ranging from tiny single-celled protozoa *Plasmodium* species that cause malaria to enormous tapeworms. Malaria is by far the most devastating parasitic disease, caused by a bite from an infected *Anopheles* mosquito.

Less devastating but far more revolting are worms such as tapeworms, which grow up to 9m (almost 30ft) long and live for up to 20 years. The dramatically named *Dracunculus* nematode (also known as a Guinea worm) grows to 1m (3ft) long. If its head peeks out, you mustn't pull it off as it can leak a powerful antigen that can trigger anaphylactic shock and death. Instead, it must be wound onto a stick and gently removed a few centimetres every day.

7.04 Demodex mites (Trigger Warning)

O h, God. You're really, really not going to like this.

Demodex folliculorum are tiny eight-legged arachnid mites that live inside hair follicles, mainly on your face. Most adults have 0.7 mites per cm² (0.16 sq in) of facial skin, although if you suffer from rosacea you're likely to have many more – around 12.8 per cm² (0.16 sq in). **You almost certainly have them crawling in, on and around you right now, although at a maximum length of 0.4mm (0.02in) it's rare to see them**. They live for around two weeks, travel mostly at night to mate (clocking up a maximum speed of 8–16mm/0.3–0.6in per hour) and then squeeze back into your hair follicles to lie, head-down, feeding throughout the day. They eat follicle cells and oily sebum from sebaceous glands in hair roots, and generally prefer the juicier hairs in your eyebrows and eyelashes, as well as around your nose, forehead and cheeks.

If you think that's the revolting bit, brace yourself. **Demodex mites have no anus**. On the upside, that means they don't poo on your face all day. On the downside, their abdomen just gets bigger and bigger until they die and disintegrate, dumping all their faeces onto you in one big splurge.

Thankfully, the mites rarely cause disease. They are associated with the skin condition rosacea, but it's unclear if they cause it or just breed better on people who have it.

7.05 Crabs, lice & nits (Trigger Warning)

Pubic crabs

Pubic crabs aren't crabs at all but rather ugly crab-like *Pthirus pubis* hairy lice that live exclusively on humans, taking four to five meals of blood every day and growing to 1.3–2mm (0.05–0.08in) long. After reaching their adult stage, they survive for about a month, busily laying an egg or so every day. They're mainly found in pubic hair because their claws are specially adapted to its thickness, but they can also live in the perianal region between your genitals and anus, and can survive in many other areas of hairier men. Their saliva is very irritating to human skin, so if you are unfortunate enough to suffer an infestation, you are likely to have a very itchy undercarriage. The good news is they rarely cause disease. Woo.

Pubic crabs are usually spread by sexual intercourse. At a stretch you might be able to blame a shared towel or bed linen but this will, quite rightly, result in raised eyebrows from friends and lovers. If you find out you are infected, you'll need a painful session with a nit comb followed by a 10-day course of lice-killing medication. Then it's time for those difficult phone calls informing all your recent sexual partners about the fun news.

Body lice

The body louse *Pediculus humanus humanus* grows up to 4mm (0.2in) long, and is usually found in people who live in close proximity to others and where good hygiene is compromised. Person-to-person contact is often to blame but poverty is invariably the root cause. The lice live and breed on clothes but visit the human body several times a day to feed on blood. Females lay up to eight eggs a day. Unlike pubic crabs, body lice transmit disease, including typhus. They bite the skin, causing itchy rashes that easily worsen and become infected. Treatment mainly involves improving hygiene – washing the body and clothes – but pediculicides (lice-killing medications) can be used if necessary.

Nits

One of the joys of owning a child is turning up at school the morning after receiving the 'someone in your class has nits' newsletter and staring into the eyes of each parent to see who looks most guilty. Invariably it's you. Head lice are 2–3mm (0.08–0.1in) long and incapable of hopping or flying. They can, however, attach their legs to the base of hair shafts and have evolved immunity to many lice-killing treatments. They can also survive being immersed in water for a long time, although wetting your hair stops them from moving. Combing them out is the best (but most painful) way to deal with them, but you'll end up going to the chemist and buying the expensive treatments whatever your doctor tells you. That's what parents do.

7.06 Bedbugs (Trigger Warning)

Cimex lectularius insects (or *Cimex hemipterus* if you're in the tropics) aren't particularly nice. They feed exclusively on human blood while you're asleep and live surprisingly long and fertile lives, with females able to lay two to three eggs a day. They aren't particularly small at 1–7mm (0.04–0.3in) but during the day they hide in crevices in and around the bed, waiting for darkness before crawling out to feed. They prefer dark, warm environments to crawl out of and feed in.

Bedbugs can carry around 30 human pathogens including MRSA, although it's not clear if they transmit any of them to us. Their bites, however, can lead to skin rashes, blisters and allergic reactions. If the bites become itchy, intense scratching can break the skin and lead to secondary problems such as infection. One particularly unpleasant problem associated with bedbugs is delusional parasitosis – a persistent hatred and fear of being infested with parasites accompanied by psychogenic itching known as tactile hallucinations.

You can try replacing mattresses and bedding, washing bedclothes at a very high temperature and vacuuming everything in sight, but bedbugs are almost impossible to eradicate. **Part of their resilience is down to the fact that adult bedbugs can survive up to six months without eating**. As a result, treatment is focused on the symptoms rather than getting rid of them. You probably need to learn to make friends with your bedbugs rather than try to kill them.

7.07 Insects that lay eggs in us! (Trigger Warning)

I wish I could tell you that spiders can lay eggs inside humans but annoyingly it's completely untrue. However, the parasitic infestation of humans by fly larvae does happen. It's called myiasis and the main culprits are botflies, screwflies and blowflies. Infestation is most common in rural tropical areas and happens through a variety of methods. Cutaneous myiasis is caused by flies laying eggs in open wounds, and can be a serious problem associated with war-related injuries in tropical areas. Larvae can also infect your body via contaminated food and by entering the mouth, nose or ears (in particularly bad aural myiasis cases, larvae can end up getting into the brain). Ophthalmomyiasis is a horrible larvae infestation of the eye, often caused by botflies.

The eggs hatch a day or so after the fly lays them on the host, producing larvae that cut into the skin and bury into the subcutaneous tissue. The lesions this creates are likely to become infected and the host has a high risk of developing sepsis or other bloodstream infections.

Chapter 08:
Weird Senses

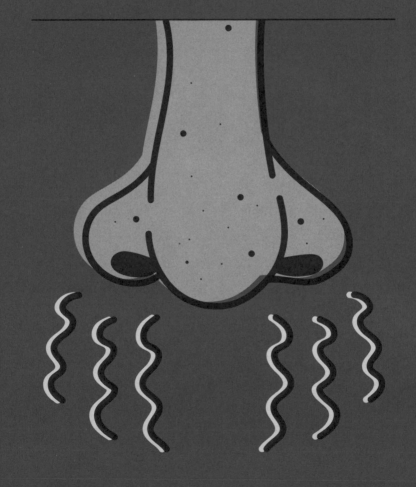

8.01 Sensory perception & embarrassment

Our embarrassment about our bodily functions is built on the machinery of sensory perception: a set of tools that serves as the interface between our brain and the outside world. The most obvious senses are sight, touch, hearing, smell and taste, although you can also sense pain, heat, time (though not very well), acceleration, balance, oxygen and carbon dioxide levels in your bloodstream as well as proprioception (the sense of movement and position of your limbs and muscles). Can you climb steps without looking at your feet? That's proprioception.

All this sensory information is sent to the brain: a silent, little-understood* organ with the consistency of Spam. You never get to see it and it never gets to see the world around you, yet it analyzes all these inputs and creates your entire sense of self, love, joy, pain, shame, faith, fear, doubt and much more.

Hear yourself fart in public and get embarrassed? That feeling is generated by your brain's pregenual anterior cingulate cortex. We don't understand the mechanism yet but most psychologists agree that embarrassment likely evolved to maintain social order and that it's revealed in classic reactions such as blushing, face-touching, downward gazing and controlled smiling, which communicate to others that we recognize and regret disrupting social norms,

*We do know that the brain is constantly fizzing with tiny electric signals that send, store and analyze information via 86 billion nerve cells called neurons, as well as 100 trillion synapses (the connections between neurons – each neuron is connected to up to 10,000 others by synapses), and 85 million non-neuronal glial cells. It uses 400 calories a day (that's 20% of your total energy use) and, interestingly, this amount stays the same whether you are concentrating hard on writing a popular science book or quietly staring at a candle flame in gloriously catatonic meditation.

thereby reinforcing them. Research shows that people who display embarrassment are more prone to be liked, forgiven and trusted than those who don't. It must have been a useful tool to help our social species to evolve but I worry that it also keeps us in our place and discourages uniqueness.

Senseology

We don't all sense the world the same way. Synaesthesia is an unusual perception of senses that allows some people to see music, letters of the alphabet or days of the week as colours. Others might associate certain sights with smells or certain words with tastes. One study indicates that around 4.4% of people are synaesthetes.

Even more fascinating are the senses other animals have that we can only dream about. Dogs sense the earth's magnetic field using magnetoreception and have a tendency to align their bodies north–south to poo. Cattle do the same. Some snakes have infra-red vision, and some bees, birds and fish can see deep into the ultraviolet frequency, beyond our visible spectrum, which effectively means they are experiencing an entire colour that we can barely conceive of. Trippy.

8.02 Body odour

Each of us is surrounded by our own unique cloud of smells that functions like a gaseous fingerprint: most of us can identify close relatives by smell, and parents can usually identify their children by smelling their clothes. Your smell changes depending on your state of health (diabetics can sometimes smell fruity or acetone-like) and dogs can diagnose a surprising range of illnesses, including COVID-19, and even epileptic fits before they happen just by sniffing you.

Humans also have clear smell preferences related to sexual selection. Researchers asked a group of women to sniff T-shirts that male subjects had slept in (the men had been assessed according to a set of specific personality traits and strictly banned from smoking, drinking alcohol or using perfumes) and then asked them to match the T-shirts to those personality traits. It turns out that women are surprisingly accurate at identifying male extraversion, neuroticism and dominance by smell alone. Dominance is thought to be associated with higher levels of certain hormones that break down into smell-influencing molecules and studies suggest women prefer men who smell more 'dominant', especially when they're at the most fertile stage of their menstrual cycle. Bizarrely, women can even identify elements of a man's body shape from smell, preferring the aroma of more symmetrical bodies (which may be a sign of genetic quality).

Researchers in Sydney found that when men eat fruit and vegetables, women think their sweat smells better 'with more floral, fruity, sweet and medicinal qualities'. The famous 'sweaty T-shirt study' by Swiss biologist Dr Claus Wedekind also discovered that women are more attracted to men whose smell suggests they have a different immune system to their own, which makes a lot of sense: any children the pair have in the future will inherit their immune systems from two very different individuals, giving them stronger defences against infection and a better chance of survival.

And men? Their smell preferences seem to have been studied a lot less, but research does show that they tend to prefer the smell of women who are ovulating and find that of menstruating women less appealing.

Odourology

Everyone knows that sweat makes us smelly but the weird thing is that sweat itself doesn't smell. Instead, a combination of three glands produces the right ingredients and damp environment for bacteria to grow, and it's these bacteria that create most of the stink. Although you sweat from every part of the body, most of your smells are cooked up in your warm, cozy parts – mainly the ones packed with glands that ooze various juices, especially in the armpits, but also in the groin, scalp, feet, mouth, perianal area and genitalia.

After these glands have oozed their juices on to your skin, the various bacteria and fungi living on you feed on them and multiply, especially in the warm, moist, relatively airless parts of our bodies covered by hair or where skin rests against skin. Our BO smell is a by-product of their activity and its chemistry is fascinating: it's a cocktail mainly comprising fatty acids, sulfanyalkanols and smelly steroids.

There's vinegary propionic acid created by propionibacteria, cheesy-fruity isovaleric acid, rancid-buttery butyric acid and eggy thioalcohols.

Interestingly, men's BO tends to smell more cheesy, whereas women's is more oniony, probably due to men's higher population of *Corynebacterium jeikeium* and women's higher population of *Staphylococcus haemolyticus*.

So, is BO bad? Well there's nothing medically wrong with being smelly but it often hints at bad hygiene, which can be problematic: being too dirty could mean your overall microbiome (see p123) is out of balance and that certain bacteria are able to multiply enough to cause disease. BO is thought to have been a useful human evolutionary tool to help identification between groups and families, as well as playing a role in attraction and reproduction.

8.03 Bad breath

Breathing is a surprisingly robust process, performed about 400 million times in the average lifespan. Each breath you inhale contains 25 sextillion (2.5×10^{22}) molecules of oxygen, but you lose a surprising amount of fluid from exhaling – about 320ml (11fl oz) of water every day. Breathing is pretty handy, for obvious reasons, but one of its few downsides is halitosis or bad breath, which can be hugely embarrassing and hellishly difficult to self-diagnose, yet family, friends and colleagues are terrified of telling you if you have it. Halitosis is mainly caused by a bacteria-rich biofilm developing on the back of the tongue that interacts with amino acids in foods to produce smelly volatile sulphur compounds, usually as a result of bad oral hygiene. But there are many other potential causes, including dry mouth, stuck food and low-carb diets, which can create an excess of fruity ketones that are released in the breath. More alarmingly, it can be caused by a condition called black hairy tongue (see p121).

The main flavour volatiles in bad breath are remarkably similar to those in your farts (see p52), although they are usually found in different quantities, giving bad breath its unique smell. Bad breath contains up to 150 components but the main ones are: hydrogen sulphide (rotten egg), methanethiol and dimethyl sulphide (old cabbage), trimethylamine (rotten fish) and indole (flowery dog poo).

Studies show that men are affected by bad breath more often than women, and that children who breathe more through their mouths than their noses are more likely to have it. Weirdly, the term 'halitosis' was coined by the company that made Listerine mouthwash (strictly speaking it was rediscovered) and halitophobia is the fear that you have halitosis, even if you don't.

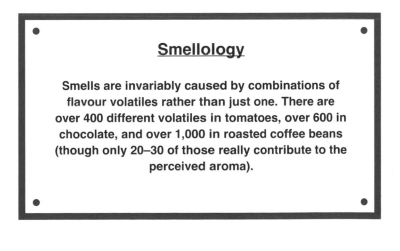

Smellology

Smells are invariably caused by combinations of flavour volatiles rather than just one. There are over 400 different volatiles in tomatoes, over 600 in chocolate, and over 1,000 in roasted coffee beans (though only 20–30 of those really contribute to the perceived aroma).

8.04 Sight

keep sheep's eyeballs in my fridge. At any one time I probably have a dozen stored in there for dissecting in my science stage shows, and they are truly fascinating, which is why I want to tell you some amazing eye facts despite there being nothing rude or embarrassing about them whatsoever. **The eye's movements are called saccades and you make around 250,000 of them every day.** All of that focusing and refocusing, along with the millions of different colours and intensities of light they take in, adds up to such a huge amount of information that a vast 30–50% of your cerebral cortex is devoted to processing it. You have a surprisingly large blind spot in each eye, although most of the time you're not aware of it because your brain fills in the missing information. You can easily find it by closing one eye, stretching your arm out as far as it will go and holding a finger up in the air. Focus straight ahead and slowly swing the finger horizontally across your arc of vision and you'll see that it disappears not far from the focal point. Keep moving the finger and it'll magically appear again.

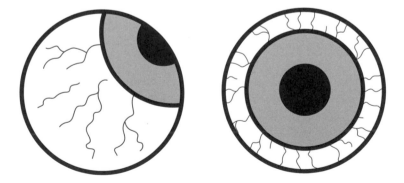

8.05 Tickling & stroking

My daughters used to regularly demand knismesis – featherlight stroking on the back of the neck or forehead – to send them to sleep (to be fair, they called it 'tickle-stroke'*). **Great white sharks like it too, and can be sent into a semi-hypnotic trance by being tickled under the snout.** Knismesis is clearly different from more boisterous laughter-inducing tickling known as gargalesis, which works with most primates (chimpanzees and gorillas make a panting sound rather than a laugh but it's thought to be the same thing). Even baby rats are tickleable.

But what's the point of tickling and stroking? Well, they both trigger the release of endorphins in the brain, which make us feel relaxed, happy and – crucially – more trusting. It's impossible to tickle yourself but the brain responds differently when someone else does the tickling. The somatosensory cortex (associated with the sense of touch) and the anterior cingulate cortex (associated with pleasure) both react more strongly when you're tickled by another person and because of this tickling is thought to be rooted in social grooming. Grooming and tickling are important physical bonding activities between children and parents, and its resultant laughter (see p60) is an important tool for releasing tension in social situations. All these elements help bind humans together, leading to better cooperation, which is crucial to social species' success.

*It's a technique I learned from my mum, who always used to make me fall asleep by gently stroking with her fingertips so that my skin tingled but didn't quite tickle. I adore being stroked like this, and when tired I often realize I'm self-stroking my forehead with the arms of my glasses. Am I weird?

You sense tickling via mechanoreceptors such as Merkel's discs, Meissner's corpuscles, Ruffini endings and Pacinian corpuscles. Light knismesis tickle sensations are felt via your slow-adapting Merkel's discs, found near the skin's surface, but gargalesis is sensed through deeper, egg-shaped Pacinian corpuscles. The mechanics for both are the same: when pressed they deform a little, sending a nerve impulse as an electric current along tiny axons (imagine impossibly small electric cables running from every nerve cell) to the brain. Meissner's corpuscles respond to fine touch and low-frequency vibrations and Ruffini endings respond to stretching.

In the late 1990s scientists also identified nerves called CT fibres that are activated by gentle stroking. These are concentrated in the head, arms, thighs and upper torso and are different from most nerve fibres, which send their information for processing in the brain's somatosensory cortex. Instead, CT fibres also send information to the insular cortex, which is used for processing emotions and has strong links to brain regions that deal with thoughts about other people and their intentions. CT fibres seem to be triggered by gentle, slow strokes of about 3–5cm (1–2in) a second and work most effectively at warm temperatures. If that ain't a tickle-stroke receptor, nothing is.

Tickleology

Experiments show that Meissner's corpuscle touch receptors, which are concentrated on hairless skin, respond to pressures of just 20mg (0.0007oz) – the weight of a fly.

8.06 Itching & scratching

tchiness is called pruritus, and the mechanism that creates the sensation is a bit of a mystery. Examining an itch point reveals little other than the usual concentration of bare nerve endings. It has similarities to the pain sensation (known as nociception) but also many differences. For instance, itching is only experienced in the outermost layers of skin, cornea or mucous membranes, unlike pain, which can be experienced deep inside the body. Also, itching makes you want to scratch whereas pain makes you want to guard or withdraw.

The itch sensation is sparked by physical touch (an insect crawling on you or fibres irritating your skin) or by chemical responses to proteolytic enzymes or histamine, but there are hundreds of causes, including allergic reactions such as hay fever and photodermatitis, skin disorders, bacterial, fungal or viral infections, and reactions to medication or disease. They're also psychogenic (originating in the mind), and I must confess that as I sit writing this I'm feeling itchy as heck.

The response to an itch is a scratch, which often feels quite delicious but is also poorly understood. Although you might think you decide whether to scratch an itch, it can sometimes be a reflex action that you have little control over. After an itch sensation is stimulated, a nearby limb – usually a hand – is automatically sent to the area and moved rhythmically to relieve the sensation. You see the same in dogs and in my cat: stroke them in a particular place and you trigger an automatic scratch response that sees their leg 'scratch' in mid-air until you stop.

Itchology

The psychological aspect of 'contagious itching', whereby just talking about itching or seeing visualizations of itchiness makes people feel itchy, isn't well understood. It may relate to the strange (and also little understood) concept of empathic 'neural mirroring', which suggests that simply watching someone else perform a physical action such as scratching an itch can trigger neural activity in your own brain that mirrors the activity that made the other person scratch themselves. This effectively replicates the sensation of the itch in you, hence itch contagion.

The gloriously named *mitempfindung*, or 'referred itch', phenomenon occurs when a sensation from one part of the body is referred to another part. In this way a scratch, itch or irritation at one place is felt somewhere completely different.

8.07 Twitching

Most muscle twitches are known as fasciculations. They can happen in any muscle but are most common in the legs and eyelids, and we don't know much about them because they're benign, so no one's really bothered studying them. We do know they are caused by an irritation in the nerves, but it's not clear where in the nerve this is activated, and in any case **twitches often occur in muscles that have not experienced any nerve irritation**. Once the irritation happens, lower motor neurons in your spine fire a signal that makes a block of muscle fibres contract. Twitches can be triggered by too little sleep or too much exercise and also correlate with overconsumption of caffeine (I suffered badly from agonizing twitching legs as a caffeine-guzzling night owl undergraduate) and magnesium deficiency.

There aren't any reliable treatments for twitches, although some epilepsy and seizure drugs may work. Lifestyle changes to improve sleep and diet usually help – though making those changes is easier said than done. I managed to cure my leg-shaking after visiting a doctor who suggested that drinking 4 litres (7 pints) of Diet Coke and eight coffees a day and always writing essays in the middle of the night, was a great route not just to twitching legs, but also to an early grave.

8.08 Yawning

For years yawning, formally known as oscitation, was one of those rare neurological quirks that we thought we understood. It was a useful tool, so the explanation went, for raising oxygen levels in the blood in response to oxygen deprivation. Then, in 1987, a paper was published that rubbished any connection between the two but offered no alternative explanation, throwing the whole world of chasmology (the science of yawning) into a state of darkness and confusion, where it remains today.

Yawning is a slow reflex action that you have lots of control over, unlike blinking, for instance, which is mainly fast and involuntary. It happens in response to boredom, tiredness and occasionally stress. We know that it increases blood flow to the skull and cools the brain slightly but we don't know if this has any significance. Weirdly, you tend to yawn most after waking from a good night's sleep.

Like smiling and laughing, yawning is highly contagious, as anyone who ever went to school knows. Even hearing someone talk about yawning can make you yawn. I'm yawning quite dramatically while writing this, and I suspect you might be yawning as you read it, too. The best explanation is that yawning is some form of empathy signal, and therefore a small but useful tool for binding social species like us together.

But **yawning is even contagious between different species**. Dogs yawn* in response to seeing humans yawning, whether they're owners or strangers, which is especially odd as we know that dogs yawn because of stress more than boredom.

*As you can discover when you read the fabulous *Dogology* (Quadrille) by little old me.

My scruffy hound Blue yawns repeatedly and dramatically (full tongue curl) during the tortuous period between me saying we're going for a walk and then us actually leaving the house after I've gathered all the necessary equipment. In other animals yawning has a wide variety of uses. Baboons yawn as a threat, penguins do it as part of their courtship ritual, and guinea pigs yawn in anger (bless 'em).

Yawnology

Babies yawn in the womb, as do people in comas. You can yawn with your mouth shut – I've done so during many a meeting – but everyone knows you're doing it because your cheeks bulge in the same way Tom Cruise's do when he's trying to act determined about something.

Chapter 09:
Body Language

9.01 Body language

We are often embarrassed, not just by the facts of our biology, but by the image we communicate to the world, and around 93% of that communication is thought to be non-verbal. In the 1960s psychologist Albert Mehrabian found that only 7% of an emotional message was conveyed by the words used to convey it. The rest came from the tone in which it is said (38%) and body language (55%). (Mehrabian said this only applied when someone was specifically talking about their likes and dislikes, but it's still pretty significant.)

Body language can be particularly embarrassing when it's used as a sexual selection tool. Feel awkward every time you step on the dance floor? It might not be your moves that are to blame. Women and heterosexual men rate the dancing of physically stronger men more highly than that of weaker men, and men assess a woman's dancing and walking as significantly sexier when she is at the most fertile stage of her menstrual cycle.

But beware: many commonly held beliefs about body language aren't as reliable as you might think. Crossed arms may give the impression that a person is defensive or angry, but can easily mean the opposite. A swaggering walk is often thought to indicate extroversion and adventurousness, and a slow, relaxed one is thought to signify calm confidence, but research shows no such correlations. It's also interesting that we are notoriously bad at identifying liars by their body language: **the ability of police, forensic psychiatrists and judges to spot lying is only slightly better than chance**.

Flirtatious female body language is traditionally thought to include touching hair, fiddling with clothes, making eye contact and nodding in agreement. But while these can all be signs of flirting, women also make the same signals with men they aren't attracted to – possibly to help them get enough information to decide if they want to take the relationship further. It turns out that flirtatious body language is only a sign of genuine interest if it continues for more than four minutes.

Even feigned body language can significantly change people's view of you. One of the classics is interview technique: holding eye contact, smiling and nodding will boost your chances in a job interview, whereas avoiding eye contact and keeping a static expression will increase your likelihood of rejection.

Feigned body language can even change your own biochemistry: a faked smile has been shown to make you feel tangibly better, and in one fascinating study psychologists told half their volunteers to hold a 'high-power' pose for two minutes, and the other half to hold a 'low-power' pose for two minutes before playing a gambling game in which the odds of winning were perfectly even. Those who held the high-power pose were much more likely to gamble and had elevated testosterone levels and decreased levels of stress-related cortisol. Your posture can also control emotions: sitting up straight creates positive emotions while sitting hunched can make you feel negative.

Beautyology

There is a strange link between your outward appearance and your temperament. Studies have shown that beautiful women are angrier than less attractive women. Your sex also has a lot of influence: men are generally angrier than women, while physically stronger men are angrier than weaker men. Young people also tend to be angrier than older people.

There's also an extraordinary correlation between immune function and perceived facial attractiveness, according to a 2021 article published in the *Proceedings of the Royal Society*. It found that perceived attractiveness in people does, indeed, correlate with health and immunocompetence. Basically, if you're attractive, you are likely to be more healthy than someone who isn't. I can't tell you how annoying I find this.

9.02 Blushing

Little is known about why we blush – Charles Darwin referred to it as 'the most peculiar and most human of all expressions'. Part of the problem is that it's immensely difficult to research. We know the mechanics: emotional stress caused by embarrassment, shyness, romantic associations or passion makes the face redden as blood flow increases in the tiny capillaries at the surface of the skin. This reddening can affect the neck, chest and ears, and make the skin feel hot or glowing.

Blushing is involuntary and so is often seen as a fundamentally honest expression of your feelings. One theory suggests that it's important for social animals like us to communicate honestly when we're ashamed (whether we want to or not) because this acknowledges that we share the same rules and values as the person who has prompted us to blush. In a sense, it's a non-verbal apology and a signal that we think in the same way as our peers, which helps with group bonding.

But blushing can get out of control, making the blusher extremely self-conscious and anxious. Just telling some people that they are blushing can cause them to blush, and extreme cases can indicate seriously problematic social phobia or social anxiety disorder.

<u>Flushology</u>

Flushing uses the same mechanics as blushing but is a different phenomenon, with a huge range of physiological rather than psychological causes. It can be caused by coughing, eating spicy food, sexual intercourse, caffeine consumption and dehydration, as well as stopping physical activity. The latter builds up blood pressure as your heart beats faster, pushing more blood through the body than is required by your muscles, resulting in very visible flushing. Drinking alcohol can trigger an alcohol flush reaction in which a build-up of acetaldehyde causes flushing in many areas of the body – 30–50% of Chinese, Korean and Japanese people are sensitive to this.

9.03 Crying

Emotional crying is a response to unhappiness, joy, anger and even happiness, but no one really knows why we do it. We get no physiological benefit from it, and we are the only animal that cries out of emotion. There are lots of theories but little consensus for various reasons, not least the wild disparities: some people don't cry at all. Charles Darwin declared emotional tears 'purposeless' and Aristotle thought that tears were a waste material like urine. **Even the idea that having a good cry brings relief isn't backed up by research**.

The most likely reason we cry is that it bolsters human sociability: crying functions as a display of vulnerability that arouses compassion in others. The evolutionary logic is that a compassionate, empathetic sensibility binds humans together and promotes cooperation, which is essential to our survival as a social species. Crying also helps neutralize anger in others (especially lovers and parents), which again is useful for a social species – though if I remember my school days correctly, it can also incite vicious taunting (though perhaps that's just Milton Keynes for you). Research shows that seeing a picture of a person crying for just 50 milliseconds inspires feelings of friendship, sympathy and supportiveness towards them.

Cryology

A 2002 study found that women cry more than men by a ratio of 2.7:1 and the international results make fascinating reading:

Country	Crying frequency per 4 weeks	
	Men	Women
Australia	1.5	2.8
Brazil	1.0	3.1
Bulgaria	0.3	2.1
China	0.4	1.4
Finland	1.4	3.2
Germany	1.6	3.3
India	1.0	2.5
Italy	1.7	3.2
Nigeria	1.0	1.4
Poland	0.9	3.1
Sweden	0.8	2.8
Switzerland	0.7	3.3
Turkey	1.1	3.6
US	1.9	3.5

Sense of shame while crying
(0 = feel no shame, 7 = I feel ashamed)

Men	Women
4.5	3.8
4.2	3.4
4.0	3.3
3.4	3.0
2.9	3.0
2.8	3.4
3.8	3.4
4.1	3.6
4.8	3.9
4.5	4.4
3.3	3.5
4.8	4.7
4.4	3.4
3.9	3.7

9.04 Frowning

The common phrase 'Turn that frown upside down' is about as welcome as a fart in a spacesuit. If I'm frowning, there's almost certainly a bloody good reason and it's wise to leave me well alone – not necessarily because I'm angry, but often because I'm concentrating. And therein lies the frown's mystery.

Frowns are created mainly by the beautifully named corrugator muscle, which pulls the brows down and together, creating horizontal 'corrugated' wrinkles across the forehead and sometimes across the bridge of the nose, too. In his book *The Expression of the Emotions in Man and Animals*, Charles Darwin referred to the corrugator as the 'muscle of difficulty' because people tend to use it when doing something mentally or physically difficult. But there's no evidence that frowning has a positive effect by helping to solve a problem. In fact, quite the opposite: research shows that making yourself frown can make you feel more negative.

It's unclear why we frown. **It isn't contagious (unlike smiling, yawning and coughing) and in fact appears to be counter-empathetic, meaning that others are less likely to be affected by the frowner's emotions**. This makes it the opposite of a social tool for binding humans together, but neither is it necessarily an expression of anger (although the corrugator is used in angry expressions, too). Along with a downturning of the corners of the mouth, frowns are also a reaction to unpleasantness.

<u>Frownology</u>

People who've had Botox injections to reduce frowning and facial wrinkles generally feel happier than those who haven't. I hate this fact.

9.05 Smiling

You have 42 different muscles in your face, allowing you to create thousands of different expressions, including 19 different types of smile. Any smile, even a fake one, is good for your soul. Research published in the *Journal of Personality and Social Psychology* shows that just pulling your face into a smile (even if you're only doing it because a researcher asked you to) can make you feel tangibly better. So the world's most annoying phrase 'Turn that frown upside down' turns out to be good advice (and consequently even more annoying).

More intriguing is the relative honesty of smiles. **Real smiles are fleeting, lasting between two-thirds of a second and four seconds**. Anything longer than that looks creepy and is unlikely to be genuine.

It's possible to distinguish between a fake 'non-Duchenne*' smile from a real 'Duchenne' smile by looking for contractions of the orbicularis oculi muscle wrapped around the eyes, which tenses the skin into crows' feet wrinkles, and the zygomatic major muscle, which pulls the lip corners upwards. Whereas the Duchenne smile uses both muscles, the non-Duchenne affects the lips and little else.

Weirdly, this isn't necessarily conscious fakery – even babies sometimes deploy non-Duchenne smiles. Five-month-olds use a Duchenne when approached by their mother, but a non-Duchenne when approached by a stranger. Happily married couples greet each other with a Duchenne smile at the end of the day whereas unhappily married couples use a non-Duchenne.

*Guillaume Duchenne was a French anatomist who first identified the wrinkly difference between a fake smile and a real one in 1862.

Non-Duchenne smiles are useful, even if they don't show genuine pleasure or enjoyment, because they can signal agreement or acquiescence. You'd think we'd be highly tuned to interpreting our fellow humans' smiles but research shows most people don't notice the difference between the two. Then again, many humans find it hard not to return a smile, even to a non-Duchenne smile.

Smiling seems far less universal than laughter, however, and some cultures use it to indicate embarrassment or confusion. In former Soviet Union countries smiling at strangers is sometimes thought odd or suspicious. I once tried smiling at a shop assistant while buying vodka in Slavutych, a Ukrainian commuter town for Chernobyl decommissioners, and far from getting even a non-Duchenne in return, I got a look of disdain that sent a shiver down my spine. Fair enough, I guess – she had no reason to be happy about a random foreigner getting drunk.

Smileology

Weirdly, women rate a man as more desirable if they see another woman smile at him. The same goes for a woman surrounded by lots of women, whether there are smiles involved or not. Men, however, are the opposite: they consistently rate a woman surrounded by men as less desirable. Aren't we pathetic?

Sources

General

Human Physiology by Gillian Pocock & Christopher D Richards (Oxford University Press, 2017)

Gray's Anatomy: The Anatomical Basis of Clinical Practice, edited by Susan Standring (Elsevier, 2020)

Anatomy, Physiology and Pathology by Ruth Hull (Lotus, 2021)

The Oxford Companion to the Body, edited by Colin Blakemore & Sheila Jennett (Oxford University Press, 2002)

02.02 Snot & bogies

'Cilia and mucociliary clearance' by Ximena M Bustamante-Marin & Lawrence E Ostrowski, *Cold Spring Harb Perspect Biol.* 9(4) (2017), a028241
ncbi.nlm.nih.gov/pmc/articles/PMC5378048/

'A guide for parents questions and answers: Runny nose (with green or yellow mucus)' (CDC)
web.archive.org/web/20080308233950/cdc.gov/drugresistance/community/files/GetSmart_RunnyNose.htm

'Rhinotillexomania: Psychiatric disorder or habit?' by JW Jefferson & TD Thompson, *J Clin Psychiatry* 56(2) (1995), pp56–9
pubmed.ncbi.nlm.nih.gov/7852253/

'A preliminary survey of rhinotillexomania in an adolescent sample' by C Andrade & BS Srihari, *J Clin Psychiatry* 62(6) (2001), pp426–31
pubmed.ncbi.nlm.nih.gov/11465519/

Sources

'PM$_{2.5}$ in London: Roadmap to meeting World Health Organization guidelines by 2030' (Greater London Authority, 2019)
london.gov.uk/sites/default/files/pm2.5_in_london_october19.pdf

02.04 Earwax
'Cerumen impaction: Diagnosis and management' by Charlie Michaudet & John Malaty, *Am Fam Physician* 98(8) (2018), pp525–529
aafp.org/afp/2018/1015/p525.html

'Impacted cerumen: Composition, production, epidemiology and management' by JF Guest, MJ Greener, AC Robinson et al, QJM 97(8) (2004), pp477–88
pubmed.ncbi.nlm.nih.gov/15256605/

02.06 Regurgitation
'Self-induced vomiting' (Cornell Health)
health.cornell.edu/sites/health/files/pdf-library/self-induced-vomiting.pdf

02.07 Pus
'What are the pathogens commonly associated with wound infections?'
medscape.com/answers/188988-82335/what-are-the-pathogens-commonly-associated-with-wound-infections

02.10 Scabs
'The molecular biology of wound healing', *PLoS Biol.* 2(8) (2004), e278
ncbi.nlm.nih.gov/pmc/articles/PMC479044/

02.11 Sweat
'Diet quality and the attractiveness of male body odor' by Andrea Zuniga, Richard J Stevenson, Mehmut K Mahmut et al, *Evolution and Human Behavior* 38 (1) (2017), pp136–143
sciencedirect.com/science/article/abs/pii/S1090513816301933

02.15 Tongue cheese

'The effect of tongue scraper on mutans streptococci and lactobacilli in patients with caries and periodontal disease' by Khalid Almas, Essam Al-Sanawi & Bander Al-Shahrani, *Odontostomatol Trop*, 28(109) (2005), pp5–10
pubmed.ncbi.nlm.nih.gov/16032940/

'Impact of tongue cleansers on microbial load and taste' by M Quirynen, P Avontroodt, C Soers et al, *Journal of Clinical Periodontology* 31(7) (2004), pp506–510
onlinelibrary.wiley.com/doi/abs/10.1111/j.0303-6979.2004.00507.x

'Tongue-cleaning methods: A comparative clinical trial employing a toothbrush and a tongue scraper' by Dr Vinícius Pedrazzi, Sandra Sato, Maria da Glória Chiarello de Mattos, Elza Helena Guimarães Lara et al, *Journal of Periodontology* 75 (7) (2004), pp1009–1012
aap.onlinelibrary.wiley.com/doi/abs/10.1902/jop.2004.75.7.1009?rfr_dat=cr_pub%3Dpubmed&rfr_id=ori%3Arid%3Acrossref.org&url_ver=Z39.88-2003

03.03 Hiccups

'Hiccups: A new explanation for the mysterious reflex' by Daniel Howes, *BioEssays* 34(6) (2012), pp451–453
ncbi.nlm.nih.gov/pmc/articles/PMC3504071/

03.06 Coughing

'ACCP provides updated recommendations on the management of somatic cough syndrome and tic cough', *Am Fam Physician* 93(5) (2016), p416
aafp.org/afp/2016/0301/p416.html

03.11 Sighing

'The science of a sigh' (University of Alberta) ualberta.ca/medicine/news/2016/february/the-science-of-sighing.html

Sources

'The integrative role of the sigh in psychology, physiology, pathology, and neurobiology' by Jan-Marino Ramirez, *Prog Brain Res* 209 (2014), pp91–129
ncbi.nlm.nih.gov/pmc/articles/PMC4427060/

04.01 Skin science
'Human skin microbiome: Impact of intrinsic and extrinsic factors on skin microbiota' by Krzysztof Skowron, Justyna Bauza-Kaszewska, Zuzanna Kraszewska et al, *Microorganisms* 9, 543 (2021)
mdpi-res.com/d_attachment/microorganisms/microorganisms-09-00543/article_deploy/microorganisms-09-00543-v2.pdf

05.02 Snogging
'A kiss is still a kiss – or is it?' (University at Albany)
albany.edu/campusnews/releases_401.htm

'Kissing in marital and cohabiting relationships: Effects on blood lipids, stress, and relationship satisfaction' by Justin P Boren, Kory Floyd, Annegret F Hannawa et al, *Western Journal of Communication* 73(2) (2009), pp113–133
scholarcommons.scu.edu/comm/9/

05.07 Belly buttons
'A jungle in there: Bacteria in belly buttons are highly diverse, but predictable' by Jiri Hulcr, Andrew M Latimer, Jessica B Henley et al, *PLoS One* 7(11) (2012), e47712
ncbi.nlm.nih.gov/pmc/articles/PMC3492386/

05.11 Human tails
'An infant with caudal appendage' by Jimmy Shad & Rakesh Biswas, *BMJ Case Rep* (2012)
ncbi.nlm.nih.gov/pmc/articles/PMC3339178/

06.02 Head hair

'The stumptailed macaque as a model for androgenetic alopecia: Effects of topical minoxidil analyzed by use of the folliculogram' by Pamela A Brigham, Adrienne Cappas & Hideo Uno, *Clinics in Dermatology* 6 (4) (1988), pp177–187

sciencedirect.com/science/article/abs/pii/0738081X88900843

06.04 Nose & ear hair

'Does nasal hair (Vibrissae) density affect the risk of developing asthma in patients with seasonal rhinitis?' by AB Ozturk, E Damadoglu, G Karakaya et al, *Int Arch Allergy Immunol* 156 (2011), pp75–80

karger.com/Article/Abstract/321912

06.06 Facial hair

'A genome-wide association scan in admixed Latin Americans identifies loci influencing facial and scalp hair features' by Kaustubh Adhikari, Tania Fontanil, Santiago Cal et al, *Nature Communications* 7, 10815 (2016)

nature.com/articles/ncomms10815

'Negative frequency-dependent preferences and variation in male facial hair' by Zinnia J Janif, Robert C Brooks & Barnaby J Dixson, *Biology Letters* 10 (4) (2014)

royalsocietypublishing.org/doi/10.1098/rsbl.2013.0958

'The role of facial hair in women's perceptions of men's attractiveness, health, masculinity and parenting abilities' by Barnaby J Dixson & Robert C Brooks, *Evolution and Human Behavior* 34 (3) (2013), pp236–241

https://www.sciencedirect.com/science/article/abs/pii/S1090513813000226

Sources

06.07 Eyebrows & eyelashes

'Supraorbital morphology and social dynamics in human evolution' by Ricardo Miguel Godinho, Penny Spikins & Paul O'Higgins, *Nature Ecology & Evolution* 2 (2018), pp956–961
nature.com/articles/s41559-018-0528-0

'The eyelash follicle features and anomalies: A review' by Sarah Aumond & Etty Bitton, *Journal of Optometry* 11 (4) (2018), pp211–222
sciencedirect.com/science/article/pii/S1888429618300487

06.08 Pubic hair

'The search for human pheromones: The lost decades and the necessity of returning to first principles' by Tristram D Wyatt, *Proceedings of the Royal Society B* 282 (1804) (2015)
royalsocietypublishing.org/doi/10.1098/rspb.2014.2994

07.01 Bacteria

'Revised estimates for the number of human and bacteria cells in the body' by Ron Sender, Shai Fuchs & Ron Milo, *PLoS Biology* 14(8) (2016), e1002533
biorxiv.org/content/10.1101/036103v1

07.07 Insects that lay eggs in us!

'Biomechanical evaluation of wasp and honeybee stingers' by Rakesh Das, Ram Naresh Yadav, Praveer Sihota et al, *Scientific Reports* 8, 14945 (2018)
nature.com/articles/s41598-018-33386-y

08.02 Body odour

'MHC-dependent mate preferences in humans' by Claus Wedekind, Thomas Seebeck, Florence Bettens et al, *Proceedings of the Royal Society B* 260 (1359) (1995)
royalsocietypublishing.org/doi/10.1098/rspb.1995.0087

'Diet quality and the attractiveness of male body odor' by Andrea Zuniga, Richard J Stevenson, Mehmut K Mahmut et al, *Evolution and Human Behavior* 38 (1) (2017), pp136–143

sciencedirect.com/science/article/abs/pii/S1090513816301933

08.03 Bad breath

'Halitosis – An overview: Part-I – Classification, etiology, and pathophysiology of halitosis' by GS Madhushankari, Andamuthu Yamunadevi, M Selvamani et al, *Journal of Pharmacy and Bioallied Sciences* 7 (6) (2015), pp339–343

jpbsonline.org/article.asp?issn=0975-7406;year=2015;volume=7;issue=6; spage=339;epage=343;aulast=Madhushankari

09.01 Body language

'More than just a pretty face? The relationship between immune function and perceived facial attractiveness' by Summer Mengelkoch, Jeff Gassen, Marjorie L Prokosch et al, *Proceedings of the Royal Society B* 289 (1969) (2022)

royalsocietypublishing.org/doi/10.1098/rspb.2021.2476

09.02 Blushing

'The puzzle of blushing' by Ray Crozier, *The Psychologist* 23 (5) (2010), pp390–393

thepsychologist.bps.org.uk/volume-23/edition-5/puzzle-blushing

Sources

09.03 Crying

'International study on adult crying: Some first results' by AJJM
Vingerhoets & MC Becht, *Psychosomatic Medicine* 59 (1997), pp85–86,
cited in 'Country and crying: prevalences and gender differences' by DA
van Hemert, FJR van de Vijver & AJJM Vingerhoets, *Cross-Cultural Research*
45(4) (2011), pp399–431
pure.uvt.nl/ws/portalfiles/portal/1374358/CrossCult_Vijver_Country_
CCR_2011.pdf

09.04 Frowning

'Facilitating the furrowed brow: An unobtrusive test of the facial feedback
hypothesis applied to unpleasant affect' by Randy J Larsen, Margaret
Kasimatis & Kurt Frey, *Cogn Emot* 6(5) (1992), pp321 338
pubmed.ncbi.nlm.nih.gov/29022461

09.05 Smiling

'Inhibiting and facilitating conditions of the human smile: a nonobtrusive
test of the facial feedback hypothesis' by F Strack, LL Martin & S Stepper,
J Pers Soc Psychol 54(5) (1988), pp768–77
pubmed.ncbi.nlm.nih.gov/3379579/

Index

Index

Acknowledgements

From as early as I can remember I watched in awe as my Dad immersed himself in books, and I desperately wanted to be like him, soaking up all the world's knowledge and stories and looking so damn clever. So, as soon as I could read I did the same, throwing myself at every book I could lay my hands on, taking a torch to bed with me every night to allow me an extra hour's reading. It didn't occur to me until much later that my Mum left the torch on my bedside table for that very purpose. I wasn't picky. I read Dostoyezsky's *Crime and Punishment* at the age of eight and, of course, I didn't have a clue what kind of pickle Raskolnikov had got himself into, but it didn't matter because I was so proud to sit there like my Dad: consuming words, hearing voices, soaking myself in stories, and it made me proud. So I want to say a huge thank you to my Dad for making me curious. If any of this book offends anyone, it's basically his fault.

A few people have kept me sane during the gestation of this pus- and vomit-stuffed manual of revolting science. Thanks to the amazing Stacey Cleworth and Sarah Lavelle and the rest of the Quadrille team. Sorry, as ever, for being perpetually late. Thanks to Luke Bird for some stunning illustrations and for simply getting it. Thanks to Daisy, Poppy and Georgia for enduring my absences – both physical and psychological. All hail the lovely team at DML: Jan Croxson, Borra Garson, Louise Leftwich and Megan Page. Thanks to Andrea Sella (Clever Fella) and all the wonderful science festival teams that have welcomed/endured me over the last 15 years. Thanks also to the legions of unnamed researchers who studied the strangest and most wonderful science with rigour and passion so I could talk about what they found and tickle you with it. And thanks, as ever, to Brodie Thomson and Eliza Hazlewood.

Thanks to Hourglass Coffee for the space to think and create, as well as some killer brews (with an extra jug of hot milk on the side).

And lastly, thanks so much to the brilliant audiences who've come along to my shows and laughed their pants off along with the Gastronaut team whilst we've explored some utterly revolting science live on stage. I LOVE you people!

Publishing Director: Sarah Lavelle
Head of Design: Claire Rochford
Designer and Illustrator: Luke Bird
Commissioning Editor: Stacey Cleworth
Copy Editor: Nick Funnell
Assistant Editor: Sofie Shearman
Head of Production: Stephen Lang
Production Controller: Nikolaus Ginelli

First published in 2022 by Quadrille, an imprint of Hardie Grant Publishing

Quadrille
52–54 Southwark Street
London SE1 1UN
quadrille.com

Cataloguing in Publication Data: a catalogue record for this book
is available from the British Library.

ISBN: 978 1 78713 640 3
Printed in China